Teaching Inside the Walls

Teaching Inside the Walls

Copyright © 2018 by Gary J. Rose, Ph.D. All rights reserved.

No part of this publication may be reproduced, stored in a retrieval system, or transmitted in any form or by any means, digital, electronic, mechanical, photocopying, recording, or otherwise, or conveyed via the Internet or a website without prior written permission of the publisher, except in the case of brief quotations embodied in critical articles and reviews.

ISBN: 978-0-9988777-5-4 (hardback)
       978-0-9988777-6-1 (paperback)

Printed in the United States of America

Teaching Inside the Walls

Teaching At-risk Incarcerated Students
Alternative Education
A Practitioners Guide to Teaching
At-Risk Students

By
Gary J. Rose, Ph.D.

*"We can't help everyone,
but everyone can help someone."*

—Ronald Reagan

TABLE OF CONTENTS

Forward 7
Acknowledgments 13
Introduction 17

So, You Want to Teach At-risk Students 33
Why Students Hate School 45
Teacher Training Programs and At-Risk Students 77
Characteristics of At-Risk Students 105
What Makes a Great Teacher?....................... 111
"Discipline Is Not a Dirty Word" 143
Accountability and Responsibility 153
How to be an Effective Teacher...................... 163
Teaching Incarcerate Adults 169
What to Teach...................................... 193
Teaching Social Skills Using Movies and Articles 201
Teaching Material/Exercises/Videos etc............... 211
Teaching with Love and Logic,
BEST, PBIS and Nurtured Hearts 289
What is Wrong with our Schools – A Commentary 303
Suggestions 317

FORWARD

by Cameron Layton

"Wish we had more teachers like Dr. Rose," were the first words from a county jail inmate on a grievance/information form. Those forms, endearingly called "kites" (as in, "Go fly a kite!") often came across my desk as I helped oversee our county inmate education program while serving as the assistant principal of a local adult school. Most of the time those 'kites' were filled with complaints or unreasonable requests of the education program. "Now that I have spent 6 weeks in his class I am simply amazed at the degree of Math he has taught me in a short 6-week program", read the rest of that student's 'kite'.

By our modern credentialing standards, Gary Rose is not a Math teacher. In the "No Child Left Behind" era, Dr. Rose would probably be considered solely a Social Science teacher. The reality, however, is that Dr. Rose is a teacher. No matter the subject or the setting, he's someone who has learned how to effectively teach anything, to anyone, at any time. He's the kind of teacher who has "amazed" me and so many others

Forward

who have crossed paths with him over the years, just as much as that inmate student.

This book is not about any one subject area, how to use assessment data, or any 'new wave' of thought. It is about how to effectively reach into the lives of struggling and resistant learners. While I served as his supervisor in our county inmate education program, I shared with Dr. Rose that our program was expected to hire teachers brave enough to enter jail classrooms and skill enough to help students learn to pass the GED exam; not an easy expectation by any stretch of the imagination.

Teaching inmates in an institution - in my opinion - represents the highest degree of challenge for an educator. A jail classroom usually does not have the ease of access to the technology and resources that are available in the typical school setting. Teachers, for the most part, are on their own by way of finding instructional material and cannot rely on accessing their favorite YouTube video or projecting the latest website to supplement their instruction. The guys and gals are in jail for several different reasons, sometimes because of violent offenses, so teachers usually cannot utilize a whole lot of partner and group work to break up class time. Classes are typically locked in for the duration; teacher preparedness is paramount. The students are adults, already years into the entrenched mindsets and bad habits they have formed, most of whom dropped out of school. There is no easy way to diagnose their education level, and most suffer from deep-seated doubts and confidence issues when it comes to learning. As one esteemed colleague, Steven Casperite, often puts it, these are "wounded learners."

Dr. Rose, with material largely purchased and organized on his own dime and own time, has gone into jail classrooms and helped students to overcome those obstacles and 'wounds' and pass the GED exam. No matter what he has been asked to teach (Math, Social Studies, English, Science), he has helped students to learn and be successful.

Success can be a very subjective term in education. Grades, attendance, opinions, even people's feelings can all come into play in determining what student success is. In the jail setting, with so many struggling, "wounded" learners facing an exam that is either passed or not passed, learning 'success' is about as black-and-white as it gets. Dr. Rose has helped the highest percentage of students pass sections of the GED exam that I have seen or heard of. But it is not just about the assessment success, it is about who has had those learning wounds healed and started to overcome those struggles - many of which have been life-long.

That is where Gary Rose has proven himself to be a master craftsman in education. As with any craft, be it medical, industrial, musical, and so on, there are years of learning and trial and error that need to take place to reach the point of mastering that pursuit. He is humble enough to admit that he has not "mastered" teaching and smart enough to share that no one has, but he is a master teacher. I do not use that word lightly, as I have seen and been around

Forward

many tremendous teachers throughout my life. My dad, a retired teacher who was undoubtedly a master of this craft, dealt with struggling learners his whole career. He, like Dr. Rose, would express that teaching struggling learners is a 'calling'. Take from that term what you may, but I would argue that not anyone can do it - at least not successfully. Most find out right away, often through shock and frustration, that facing classrooms full of struggling learners and trying to drive them to success takes a unique person, with a unique level of patience, creativity, understanding, determination and passion.

Later in this book, Dr. Rose references a quote from Mike Singletary; "Don't tell me, show me." During my ten years as a continuation high school teacher and coach, I learned that is what so many struggling students needed from me. I could talk all day, wow them with presentations and displays, and utilize the best technology and curriculum, but if I did not find out how to show my students what they needed to learn, they so often would not get it. "Those students" need us to work hard, work smart, and to show that we care enough to show them how to learn and rise above their struggles. Having spent the majority of my career face-to-face with struggling, resistant learners, I know that "in the trenches" mentality is how we have to function.

This book, which provides invaluable insight from a proven master educator, hits on all four of the qualities mentioned previously: patience, creativity, understanding, and determination. Dr. Rose states,

Gary J. Rose, Ph.D.

reflecting on his first move towards public education, "I felt that maybe I could make a difference." He can now remove the word "maybe", as he has definitely made a difference in so many lives.

I remember a number of students at my continuation high school years ago, talking about their time in and out of our local juvenile hall. It was fascinating to me that nearly every time they shared their experiences, their stories involved a teacher named Dr. Rose. Kids who often spent most of their time fronting and bragging about how tough they were, and how they could care less about school, would be boasting about how much they had learned during their week or month or longer in the "Hall." I heard things like "Oh, Dr. Rose is SO legit... he's the best teacher!", or "Yeah, Rose taught me more than anyone else ever has!" I was blown away that instead of sharing what landed them in the "Hall," how bad the food was, or the terrible "grandpa shoes" they had to wear while in custody, they would be most excited about spending time in classes with Dr. Rose.

I spent a number of years wondering who this miracle worker was, and - honestly - a little jealous of him. Not too many years later I received a phone call from Gary Rose, inquiring about an inmate education opening at our adult school. Not until sitting down with him at an impromptu meeting in my office did I realize that this was "the" Dr. Rose. We reminisced about the students we had shared and discussed the new focus on educating inmates - hoping and striving for education to be a catalyst for rehabilitation as the

Forward

state began to push to eliminate the "revolving door" in our jail and prison systems. He discussed then, as he does later in this book, how he makes learning "fun", "engaging", and "relevant" to reach his learners.

Far from the jargon and "edu-speak" that fills most books written for educators today, Dr. Rose's approach is to simply tell his story, full of the 'trials and errors' that led to becoming a master craftsman, and detail how he has found success with students. His goal is to fully engage his students, not just captivate them with some great story from his past, by making their learning immediately relevant and important to them. He cares far more about his students than he does about himself, his own comfort level, or what will make his life in the classroom easier. He has spent years in different classrooms working harder than most, and - more importantly - learning how to work smarter.

Dr. Rose has written this book with the same practical application and straightforward language that he uses with his students. He tells stories, shares insight, provides context and bullet points, and - through it all - shares a lifetime of learning how to be successful with struggling and resistant learners. My hope is that both those currently working in classrooms, as well as those moving in that direction, will read this book and pull from it the invaluable experience, wisdom and practical skills that Dr. Rose lays out.

Cameron Layton
Assistant Principal, Lincoln High School

ACKNOWLEDGMENTS

In 2018, it is estimated that there are 3.5 million certificated teachers in the United States. Several of them could easily be candidates as the best in their field. To those dedicated educators, I salute you. I believe that you are recognized as the best in your area due to your dedication to your students, continually looking for new, more exciting material to make your classes come alive.

It is safe to say, however, that none of these candidates practice the specific teaching of the 50,000 plus U.S. students (juveniles and adults) who attend school behind bars.

So, besides dedicating this book to my mother, who placed a high standard for the rest of our family regarding giving our best in everything we do, I want to acknowledge those teachers who inspired and taught me how to teach "at-risk" students. These teachers, in no set order, are:

E.R. Braithwaite, Jaime Escalante, LouAnne Johnson, Ron Clark, and Joe Clark.

E. R. Braithwaite, famed for his 1959 autobiographical novel later displayed in the 1967 film *To Sir With Love*,

Acknowledgments

illustrated, although somewhat simplistically, how to deal with unruly, rude, disrespectful students from dysfunctional families in Great Britain. The term, "at-risk" students, was not used in education in 1959. Realizing that he was not bonding with his students, Mr. Tackary, played by Sidney Poitier, abandons most of the required curriculum and instead begins teaching life skills for the real-life situations his students would face upon their graduation.

Next is Jaime Escalante, who had a significant impact on my desire to enter the teaching profession. The book *Escalante – The Best Teacher in America* (Jay Mathews – ISBN 0-8050-1195-1) describes in greater detail, how Mr. Escalante challenged his students to study AP Calculus and then, after being accused of cheating, encouraged his students to retake the exam, showing that they did not cheat on the first exam. This book, like Braithwaite's novel, "To Sir with Love," was also parlayed into the highly successful film, Stand and Deliver.

LouAnne Johnson, in her book, *My Posse Don't Do Homework* (ISBN 10: 031207638), also inspired me with several techniques she used with her "at-risk" students after realizing that what she learned in her teaching college would have little relevance with the individuals in her classroom. Like *To Sir with Love* and *Stand and Deliver*, LouAnne Johnson's book was made into a major motion picture, Dangerous Minds. Although she admits that the film is "loosely" based on actual events, I found her later book Teaching

Gary J. Rose, Ph.D.

Outside the Box (ISBN 3: 978-1119089278) answers the essential questions that you face as an educator—how to engage students, encourage self-directed learning, differentiate instruction, and create dynamic lessons that nurture critical thinking and strategic problem solving.

Ron Clark, working with "at-risk" middle schoolers, proposed fifty-five essential rules for success in and out of the classroom, many of which focus on respect and school policies. In other words, he taught his "at-risk" students, life skills. These included making eye contact, respect others' ideas and opinions, always be honest, and be the best person you can be". He later proposed eleven traits of excellence: enthusiasm, adventure, creativity, reflection, balance, compassion, confidence, humor, common sense, appreciation and resilience.

Mr. Joe Clark, who, in his book *Laying Down the Law: Joe Clark's Strategy for Saving Our Schools*, explained steps he used to clean up Eastside High School in Paterson, New Jersey, and how his prescription for reform could be duplicated by parents and principals working together to clean up their neighborhood schools. His famous quote, "Discipline is not the enemy of enthusiasm," where he summed up my philosophy on discipline that I still used today with my incarcerated "at-risk" inmates.

Finally, to the men and women of the Milpitas Police Department. When I receive accolades about my teaching abilities, I always state that what made me a better teacher, teaching "at-risk" students, came

15

Acknowledgments

from the training and experience I received while a member of our police department. The training/teaching I received from my field training officer, Ed Cardoza, planted the seed that would eventually grow into a teacher of "at-risk" incarcerated students.

INTRODUCTION

How did I become an educator of "at-risk" incarcerated students?

During my employment as a police officer, I experienced the art of teaching. It became a calling. After serving time in our undercover unit, the chief of police felt it necessary for me to spend time in our community relations division as part of my transition back to the street. In that capacity, part of my responsibility was to teach grade-level subjects to students in our elementary schools, junior high (middle school) and our high school.

Kindergartners were taught Dangerous Strangers: Red Light/Green Light. Second graders would receive a lesson on bike safety and crossing streets. Fourth graders were introduced to laws such as vandalism and shoplifting, while six-graders were taught about consequences for violating bike thefts, burglary, drugs and alcohol.

Personally, I did not feel I was teaching. Instead, I was performing a dog and pony show. I would stand in front of them in my uniform and watch them continue to focus on my firearm and baton. I must say that in the early grades it was nice to be perceived as a hero

While teaching in the elementary grades, I learned quickly that few students have a grasp on the difference between a question and a story. I recall on many occasions during Q&A period, that instead of getting a question, I got more information than I needed to know.

"My dad got arrested for drunk driving and my mom took me and my sister to a motel."

"My parents roll their own cigarettes in bed and it stinks when they smoke."

Being perceived as a hero while teaching in the younger grades, would not be the perception while teaching some older students in the junior high and high school level. In those grades, some students already had run-ins with the police creating a negative feeling towards law enforcement. Some had been place on informal probation (reporting to a juvenile officer of the Milpitas Police Department) or had been formally charged with a crime and incarcerated in juvenile hall. Being placed on probation, they did not see me as a "hero" but just as "the man."

My first real "teaching" assignment when compared to a traditional teacher, started when I was assigned two classes at our high school where I would teach Introduction to Criminal Justice. Students had to either a junior or senior to attend. I had to create lesson plans, methodologies, and while on campus, had to perform as a typical high school teacher. This was brand new to me, but I relished the experience.

While teaching for those two years at our high school, I began to understand what an educator's role was, and the awesome responsibility they have in the education of our children. Most students want to learn, and during the 1980's, when I first started teaching, most desired to advance onto colleges or universities. Although I rarely interacted with my student's parents, I would always receive requests from many of them, regarding the progress of their child; something that will rarely happen with at-risk students and their parents/guardians.

As much as I enjoyed my time as a part-time educator, my love was still that of a police officer and upon completing my two years, I went back to the patrol division. I continued moving up the ranks, culminating in the rank of sergeant. I was content in serving my community.

In addition to in-service training I was honored to be selected as one of two sergeants from our department, to receive training in a newly developed specialist designation of hostage negotiator. Before to the development of hostage negotiations, most departments had a fully functional SWAT (Special Weapons and Tactical Teams) to handle barricaded suspects, with or without hostages. It wasn't until Dr. Harvey Schlossberg of the New York Police

Introduction

Department, put together that city's first hostage negotiation team, that hostage negotiation became vogue. Now, police agencies could use trained hostage negotiators, to resolve these tense situations, without having to use lethal force as the only avenue or response.

I point this out, since I feel that much of my success as a teacher of both juvenile and adult incarcerated individuals, was due to this psychological training I received from both Dr. Harvey Schlossberg and later, from the San Francisco Police Department. Fast forward to 2017, and I am glad to see that many agencies, in addition to hostage negotiation teams, have teams of officers, who respond to crisis situations before it escalates into a full-blown hostage situation.

My first book, a rendition of my doctoral dissertation entitled *"Towards the Integration of Police Psychology Techniques to Combat Juvenile Delinquency in K-12 Classrooms,"*

(ISBN 9781493556953) points out the advantages former law enforcement officers and military personnel have, interacting with "at-risk" individuals, largely due to their training. In my dissertation (and in my book) I outlined the various causes for juvenile delinquency and how newly trained teachers are ill prepared to face "at-risk" students in their classrooms due to a lack of instruction in our teacher colleges. I will address some of these issues in this book, but since my first book was a doctoral dissertation, it contains a tremendous amount of citations that a reader can use to explore further.

In 1987, after sustaining a career ending industrial injury, I retired from the Milpitas Police Department. I left behind a lot of great colleagues, memories, that I will never forget. But it is because of these interactions with my former colleagues, memories and experiences, as well as the training I received that, prepared me for my next career. That would be an educator of "at-risk" students.

I'm asked many times why, after retiring from law enforcement, I entered the role of a teacher - and not just a teacher, but a teacher of "at-risk" students. Part of my decision is based on my type-A personality and after "trying" to retire, found that it was not for me. I could not return to law enforcement due to my disability, but I remembered with fondness, how much I enjoyed teaching at the high school level. So, I began exploring this new arena.

Secondly, I was shocked at the performance of our students here in California, on what use to be called the STAR test, when compared to the other forty-nine states. This type of testing ended in 2013, but at that time, the results were shocking.

Has it gotten better?

In a 2018 study, U.S. News (Best States) Education Rankings, listed California #41 in the nation. The largest state in the union and we are in the middle of the pack.

Introduction

States Ranking

1. Massachusetts
2. New Hampshire
3. New Jersey
4. Vermont
5. Connecticut
6. Maine
7. Minnesota
8. Iowa
9. Rhode Island
10. Montana
11. Pennsylvania
12. Virginia
13. Maryland
14. Illinois
15. Nebraska
16. Wisconsin
17. Indiana
18. Delaware
19. Missouri
20. Utah
21. Michigan
22. South Dakota
23. North Carolina
24. Kentucky
25. Idaho
26. Washington
27. Kansas
28. North Dakota
29. Tennessee
30. Colorado
31. New York
32. Hawaii
33. Texas
34. Wyoming
35. Georgia
36. Ohio
37. Oregon
38. Arkansas
39. Alabama
40. Florida
41. West Virginia
42. Oklahoma
43. South Carolina
44. **CALIFORNIA**

California placed 44th in literacy and 41st in mathematics

I could not believe that our students were more deficient than their counterparts in the other states. How could California, having one of the highest tax bracket in the United States, have students performing so poorly? After entering the teaching profession, I got a dose of reality of what, in my opinion, was causing the problem which I will allude to later.

Third, I felt that maybe I could make a difference. I am a realist and know that one person is not going to change the educational philosophy of the State of California. But, like my former students (cadets) who attended the Alder Grove Academy and the subject of my book "*Hitting Rock Bottom*," I felt that if I could help at least one student achieve their success academically, I was giving something back to society.

Those were the reasons I left retirement and entered the role of a teacher of at-risk students. Initially I only desired to be a substitute teacher, but after I jumped through all the hoops set up by the State of California Department of Education regarding credentialing, my first supervisor felt that I would be a great fit, due to my prior law enforcement career, to teach full-time in our county's juvenile hall. Little did I know at the time, but this new career would span over 20 years, longer than my career in law enforcement.

This book will define what Alternative Education is and the common characteristics "at-risk" students, both juveniles and adults, will display when they are assigned to your class should you decide to become a teacher of "at-risk" students. I will be speaking in

Introduction

generalities since each school district and student is unique, but I have found in over 20 years teaching "at-risk" students in various alternative education facilities, that my methodologies have been successful and most students thrive under such tutelage.

I wanted to start my career as a teacher by "hit the ground running." I researched for books on how to teach "at-risk" incarcerated youth, but found very little "how to do it," books. Most books were based on theory or what the "experts" call best practice. That was all fine and good, but how was this going to help me when little Johnny tells me to "f--- off?"

Now that I am closer to the end of my career as a teacher of "at-risk" incarcerated students than the beginning, I feel that there is a definite need for a "how-to-book." Statistics tell us that more and more teachers leave the profession within two years. The reason, classroom management issues. Just as each student is unique, so is each teacher. Some of the recommendations I make may not be suitable to your location, your personality and so on. Since we all have different personalities, temperaments, tolerance/stress levels, experience and training, "one size does not fit all." Some of you are veteran teachers while others are new to the teaching profession, especially in the alternative education arena. Hopefully there will be something for everyone.

In subsequent chapters, I will describe the various facilities where I taught; the support personnel (if any), administration philosophies I had to work under; types of students and their characteristics; methodologies and strategies; and material I have used over the decades.

You, the reader, can pick and choose what methods, strategies and material you may want to implement; deciding on whether to use the same material, or modify/ re-create new context that will fit with your personality, methodology and students.

Over my 20 years teaching "at-risk" incarcerated students, I have witnessed many of the changes in education that have been recommended by "consultants" and think-tanks, integrated into our classrooms. These include behavioral programs such as BEST, Nurtured Hearts, PBIS, and Teaching with Love and Logic. I will explain the philosophies of each program and the goals each program hoped to accomplish.

I will discuss my philosophy regarding classroom management and my bias for and against these behavioral programs and what I have found that works best with "at-risk" students. In this regard, a quote by former principal Joe Clark will give you a hint as to my philosophy in advance, when he stated that, "Discipline is not the enemy of enthusiasm."

In another chapter, I will list several videos and exercises that I have used over the years to emphasize a learning module whether it was for U.S. or World history, geography, English language arts, U.S. Government, Science, Economics, Literature, and

Introduction

what exercises I have asked my students to perform after viewing such films.

While teaching at our county's juvenile detention facility, I read the book, *Escalante – The Best Teacher in America* (Jay Mathews) and viewed the hit movie *Stand and Deliver* – both of which impacted my career as an educator. You can imagine how thrilled I was when I received an invitation to personally meet Jaime Escalante during an awards presentation where he was the recipient.

In a one-on-one meeting, Mr. Escalante asked me where I taught. When I replied, "At our county's juvenile hall," he responded, "Good, the bad boys and girls – they deserve a good education also." In our conversation, he went on to say that during his teaching career he rarely found a single stand-alone textbook. Instead, he recommended that all good teachers continue to search for new, better, and more relevant material to be incorporated into their curriculum, thus making their presentation more exciting and fresh. You will hear me refer to those sentiments throughout this book.

I do not profess to have all the answers regarding the teaching of "at-risk" students assigned to alternative education programs including incarcerated adults customarily serviced by adult education departments. I offer this book and my thoughts merely as suggestions and strategies that worked for me, in hopes that you too will find success using such tactics while instructing your students.

Gary J. Rose, Ph.D.

There is no better feeling than running into one or your former "at-risk" students some day in the future, and having them say, "thank you for being my teacher and helping me straighten out my life. If it weren't for you, I would be in prison or dead." You will encounter many successes along the way, but also some students that just "don't get it." A close friend and fellow teacher, saw on television, a former student being cuffed and arrested for killing a California Highway Patrol officer. He said to me, "you can't save them all," and that is the best advice I can give you. Some will break your heart.

I sincerely hope you get something out of this book that you can use, even if it is just some new inspiration, and wish you all the success in the world in your career. Some say that you will not have many rewards working with "at-risk" students in alternative education since you cannot compete with what traditional schools offer such as baseball, football, basketball and cheerleading teams, including auto shop, welding, arts and crafts. That is true, and as close as you might become with your "at-risk" students, you must encourage them to return to their traditional schools. But as I have stated, years later, your at-risk students will never forget you because you took the time and made the commitment in turning their lives around. Don't expect being recognized for your work with "at-risk" students. In my career of 15 plus year working with my colleagues in the alternative education division, specifically with incarcerated

Introduction

juveniles or court and community schools, not one colleague ever won the "teacher of the year award." That honor is generally reserved for traditional school teachers. But if you truly want to make a difference in society, think about how rewarding it will be to work with students that others have given up on, and help them turn their lives around. To me, this is much more satisfying that winning a "teacher of the year award" especially when you run into them someday and find that they are now squared away, have a family, good job, shelter, and a positive attitude on life, and realize that you had a hand in helping them get there.

As rewarding as it has been teaching and making an impact on "at-risk" student's lives, be prepared for those students that fail and tear your heart out. Case in point.

On November 17, 2005, a California Highway Patrol Officer made a car stop near Woodland, California. Almost immediately, after the driver rolled down his window, a shot rang out taking the life of the officer. The suspect and his girlfriend fled the scene leaving the officer to die on the roadway.

The next day, while at home recovering from another knee surgery, a fellow teacher and I were watching a local news station on television when the normal program was interrupted with an update over the search of the cop killer.

I was shocked when I saw the killer handcuffed and being escorted to a patrol car. He was one of

Gary J. Rose, Ph.D.

my former "at-risk" students I taught at our county's juvenile detention facility.

This student entered my life when I met him in the A-Unit ward of the Placer County Juvenile Detention facility. Prior to our first meeting, a probation officer asks to speak with me privately. He informed me that this student's father had been a police officer in Los Gatos, California the same time I was employed with the Milpitas Police Department. His father was later fired for bad decision making and, now, tainted as a "bad cop," could not find a job. So, he became a bank robber.

During his last heist, he was confronted by the police upon his exit from the bank. Refusing to be arrested, he shot himself, dying at the scene. This event obviously left a lasting impress on my student. The probation officer wanted me to not only have this knowledge but hoped that it might help me bond with this student who seemed to be an introvert.

I called the student aside and introduced myself. I informed him that I had been a police officer at the same time as his father, but did not know him. I then said that when we are born, we do not have a hand in determining who our parents might be, but regardless, an individual must determine for themselves what road they will travel, especially as they enter adulthood. The student seemed to agree with my assessment of life, yet was constantly a returning student incarcerated in juvenile hall for various law violations. Upon reaching

Introduction

adulthood, I lost track of him, yet always hoped that he had eventually turned his life around.

For whatever reason, I could not accept the fact that I somehow did not bond with this student. Was there something else I could have done to change his life that would have influence future events and saved the life of the California Highway Patrol officer? I needed an answer to this question since it was constantly nagging at me.

In October 2014, I arrived outside the walls of San Quentin Prison in Marin County. I had received permission from this student to visit him on death row. Several letters had been exchanged between us and he knew why I was there.

After enduring numerous security checks, I found myself seated on a chair looking through a thick glass window into a small unoccupied cubicle. The clanging of doors, cat-calls, movement of inmates created nervous energy in me. I kept thinking that here I was, a retired police sergeant, visiting a former student whose father had been a cop turned bank robber, and now his son was awaiting his execution for killing a law enforcement officer. Sounded like a television movie plot.

After several minutes, a door to the cubicle opened and there was my former student. He smiled at me and motioned to the communication box located to the side of the window. I pressed the button but could not find words to say. I released the button, stared at him, and tried again.

Gary J. Rose, Ph.D.

To this day, I recall exactly what I said which was not very profound. I told him that I had hoped the two-and-a-half hour drive to San Quentin, would give me enough time to know what I wanted to say, but now I am lost for words.

Using the communication device, he reminded me why I was there. To see if there was anything I could have done differently as his teacher, to not only bond with him, but might have changed the course of future tragic events. He then gave me a compliment by saying that I was the only teacher he ever had that really seemed to care about him. He thanked me for educating him to the point that he passed all four sections of the GED when he first left the juvenile detention facility and became an adult. He knew of the military-style boot camp academy I ran for the Placer County Office of Education and said that perhaps if he had had the opportunity to attend such a school, his life might have turned out differently.

Unfortunately, he said, he became addicted to meth and his life was never the same again. He would prefer execution versus the long-life incarceration he faces inside San Quentin prison, but that was all he had to look forward too.

After finishing our visit, I returned to my parked truck in the parking lot adjacent to the shoreline of San Francisco Bay. Before starting my vehicle, I listened to the small waves reach the shore and then I realized that I just left the prison and will be returning home, but that my student will only be leaving the prison in a body bag. It tore at my heart and still does today.

Fortunately, you will have numerous success stories teaching "at-risk" students, both juvenile and adult, but be prepared for the occasional unfortunate results of your good intentions and hard work.

"If we expect kids to be losers they will be losers; if we expect them to be winners they will be winners. They rise, or fall, to the level of the expectations of those around them, especially parents and their teachers."

—Jaime Escalante

SO, YOU WANT TO TEACH AT-RISK STUDENTS

What is Alternative Education? According to the National Center for Education, Evaluation and Regional Support (September 2014), there are forty-three states and the District of Columbia who have broadly defined definitions of Alternative Education as educational activities that fall outside the traditional K–12 curriculums—include homeschooling, general educational development (GED) programs, gifted and talented programs, and charter schools (Aron, 2006). Because individual states or school districts define and determine the features of their alternative education programs (Lehr, Lanners, & Lange, 2003), applications may differ in definition, target population, setting, services, and structure.

"Alternative" has had many different meanings to different people over the past several years (Characteristics of Alternative Schools, and Programs Serving At-risk Students – High School Journal, Vol.81, No.4, May 1988, pp.183-198).

Raywid (1994) noted that there was a variety of definitions concerning "alternative schools." She provided a summary of alternative definitions which she broke down into (3) types.

Type I Alternative schools are the most popular. Many resemble magnet schools. They are likely to reflect programmatic themes emphases about content or instructional strategy or perhaps both. Some charter schools would fall into this classification in that, in addition to teaching their state's academic standards (now Common Core), they would emphasize additional offerings of interest to the prospective students such as STEM (Science, Technology, Engineering, and Math), or school that attract students who have keen interest in music or art to name a few.

Type II Alternative programs are schools in which the student has been formally placed (most of the time without their consent) due to "one last chance" before expulsion. These programs utilize various behavioral modification strategies, and little emphasis is being taught on pedagogy or curriculum.

Type III Alternatives are for those students judged needing remediation or rehabilitation – academic, social/emotional, or both. The assumption is that after successful completion of treatment, the student can return to their traditional campus.

Although adult education does not fall specifically under Alternative Education, many programs offered under adult education departments, such as inmate education, have many similarities as Alternative Education programs.

In my experience and while teaching at various institutions, many programs had a mixture of all three types in their classrooms and therein is the challenge you will face. In these programs, choice, remediation, and innovation combine to address the needs of at-risk students (Raywid).

Raywid (1994) further noted that, "two enduring consistencies have characterized alternative schools from the start: they have been designed to respond to a group that appears not to be optimally serviced by the regular program, and consequently, they have represented varying degrees of departure from standard school organization, programs and environment (p.26).

Most Alternative Education schools have flexible schedules that include hours that are either expanded or shortened when compared to that district's normal school day. Many sites include the ability of a student to study for their GED either separately on in conjunction with the normal curriculum being taught. The determination of whether to pursue a GED versus a traditional high school diploma is generally decided after an examination of the time required to make up credit deficiencies needed for the traditional diploma. In addition, some students, with the concurrence of their parents, wish to finish their education quickly and opt for the GED. Others, due to criminal activity, dysfunction families, drugs/alcohol abuse and truancy, refused to go to school and once they are forced to return, are so far behind, that only a fast-track education pathway will work.

More and more students are being labeled at-risk in our public schools with an influx occurring in the 21st century. Many are assigned to Alternative Education programs due to school suspension/expulsion, falling behind academically, and truancy. Others arrived in our Alternative Education classrooms due to more serious reasons and are referred by the juvenile court system of your county and/or placed because of formal or informal probation.

In some districts/jurisdictions, Alternative Education schools are referred to as "second chance" schools, continuation schools (both middle and high school), or as independent study. Alternative Education schools were created to address the special needs of these at-risk students, that could not be offered at the traditional school site. In the case of inmate education, many counties feel that by offering incarcerated adults the opportunity to earn their GED, they would be more energized to seek either more education upon their release, but minimally, seek a good paying jobs, reducing recidivism.

Also, many Adult Education programs focus on pathways which inmates can use to visualize a goal in many trades such as health, hotel and culinary, business, and Information technology.

As Assistant Principal Steve Casperite of Placer County School for Adults states, "It's what the community needs to get people back to work. It gets people better paying jobs."

These are very achievable goals for a society to seek for our inmate populations, but the underlying problems brought to the classroom by at-risk students, (incarcerated juvenile and adults) must be addressed by you, the classroom teacher.

What else can we learn about the type of students that will make up your classroom? In a 2006 study, the "at-risk" student population and educational services offered to youth attending Alternative Education programs suggest that programs appear to be largely site-based, often operating in physical facilities with limited access to academic support. The student population appears to be predominately high school students with a large portion of students identified as disabled (emotionally).

The general education curriculum is reported as a predominant course of study among alternative schools, supplemented with vocational education. Students appear to be provided with several schools and community support activities. (Foley, Regina M. and Pang, Lang-Sze, "Alternative Education Programs:

Program and Student Characteristics" (2006) http://digitcommons.unomaha.edu/slcestgen/62.

As stated previously, when the definition of alternative education for "at-risk" students is expanded to include public alternative schools, charter schools for "at-risk" youth, programs within juvenile detention centers, community-based schools or programs operated by districts, and alternative schools witl1 evening and weekend formats, and GED programs for incarcerated adults, the number of offerings have increased substantially.

The National Center on Educational Statistics, for the academic year 2000-2001, reported 10,900 alternative public schools and programs serving 612,000 students were operating in the United States (Kleiner et al. 2002).

Alternative education programs are often viewed as individualized opportunities designed to meet the educational needs for youth identified as "at-risk" for school failure. More recently, these programs have been viewed as programs for disruptive youth who are experiencing difficulty in traditional schools (National Association of State Directors of Special Education, 1999). Likewise, the approaches and orientation of the programs appear to differ accordingly. Some programs emphasize a disciplinary orientation and others focus on developing an innovative program that seeks to meet students' unique educational needs (Lehr & Lange, 2003).

Descriptions of alternative schools and programs have suggested such programs exhibit specific structural and programming characteristics. For example, alternative education programs have often been characterized as small enrollment programs. Earlier reports have suggested the student populations of programs were approximately 200 students or less (Franklin, 1992; Lange & Sletten, 2002; Paglin & Fager, 1997).

Other descriptions have identified individualized instruction which meets students' unique academic and social-emotional needs as characteristic of alternative education programs (Franklin, 1992; Lange & Sletten, 2002). Third, supportive environments that strengthen relationships among peers and between teachers and students are often reported as a quality of alternative education programs (Franklin, 1992; Lange & Sletten, 2002).

Furthermore, youth attending alternative education programs appear to have diverse educational backgrounds and needs. This is a shared characteristic of many incarcerated adults attending GED programs. Often, youth are referred to such programs for a variety of reasons including experiencing behavioral difficulties in schools, being suspended or expelled from school, being a pregnant or parenting teen, experiencing academic failure, or having a disability. Youth who attend the programs have also been identified as being a member of an ethnic minority group (Lange & Lehr, 2003; Paglin & Fager, 1997; Raywid, 1994).

The predominant management approach governing alternative education programs appears to be site-based management. Over three-fourths of alternative education programs engaged in site-based management. One fifth used a centralized management approach for their programs. An overwhelming majority (80%) of alternative education programs operate in off-campus facilities.

A small percentage of programs utilize the same building as traditional education programs (8%) or community colleges (2%). Likewise, a majority (80%) of alternative education programs operate as a closed campus; meaning students are not allowed to leave and return during a school day. Once they arrive, they are to stay until the school time-period ends. Very few programs (16%) have open campuses (Foley, Regina M. and Pang, Lang-Sze, "Alternative Education Programs: Programs and Student Characteristics" (2006).

In the case of juvenile suspension and expulsion referrals, the student can no longer come onto the school campus or face further consequences. They must attend their assigned Alternative Education site until they complete a rehabilitation plan; in other words, met the requirements set by their traditional school before they can return.

Most of the districts in a study conducted in 2007-08, reported offering alternative schools and programs for students in grades 9 through 12 (88 to 96 percent), with offerings for grades 6 through 8 reported by 41 to 63 percent of districts, and for grades 1 through 5 by 8 to 18 percent of districts (table 5). The grades in which districts reported offering alternative schools and programs varied by district enrollment size.

There were 10,300 district-administered alternative schools and programs for "at-risk" students in the 2007–08 school year. Of these schools and programs, 37 percent were housed within a regular school. (Carver, P. R., and Lewis, L. (2010).

(Alternative Schools and Programs for Public School Students At-Risk of Educational Failure: 2007–08 (NCES 2010–026). U.S. Department of Education, National Center for Education Statistics. Washington, DC: Government Printing Office).

Cases for Referral

Districts in 2009, reported that students were transferred to an alternative school or program for physical attacks or fights (61 percent); the possession, distribution, or use of alcohol or drugs (excluding tobacco) (57 percent); disruptive verbal behavior (57 percent); continual academic failure (57 percent); chronic truancy (53 percent); the possession or use of a weapon other than a firearm (51 percent); and the possession or use of a firearm (42 percent) (Kleiner, B., Porch, R., and Farris, E. (2002). Public

Alternative Schools and Programs for Students At-Risk of Educational Failure: 2000–01 (NCES 2002–004). U.S. Department of Education. Washington, DC: National Center for Education Statistics).

Yes, these will be your students. I have found that additionally, as a compounding factor, many will come from socio-economic dysfunctional families. It is not uncommon to find one or both parents in or out of jail/prison. Many have been influenced by gangs. But the most common characteristic of at-risk students, is that they have made bad choices. With no mentor or role-model for them to admire, they turn to other students who are trapped in the same environment. Gangs offer a substitute for their dysfunctional families.

A subset of "at-risk" students, are those that I taught. These are students that have violated the law and are incarcerated consequently. It also includes the adult inmate. So, besides all the characteristics described above, add to that they are now locked up with others, many of which have similar tendencies towards "at-risk" behavior.

Please do not get me wrong. I am still a "cop" at heart, and not a bleeding-heart liberal who are shocked that we put so many people in juvenile hall, jail, or prison. *Baretta* was an American detective television series which ran on ABC from 1975 to 1978. At the beginning of each episode, Sammy Davis, Jr. sang a song which contained the motto, **"Don't do the crime, if you can't do the time."** I sometimes sang that song as well as the song by the Bobby Fuller Four, ***I Fought the Law and the Law Won*** in the classroom which may sound cruel, but later you will see, it was a bonding exercise.

As previously stated, I will not bore you with psychological or social economic stats as to what creates at-risk students. That is contained in *Towards the Integration of Police Psychological Techniques to Combat Juvenile Delinquency in K-12 Classrooms.* Instead I will move forward with why many students seem to hate school.

"Don't wait until you reached your goal to be proud of yourself. Be proud of every step you take toward reaching that goal."

WHY STUDENTS HATE SCHOOL

I recently found an excellent website that lists the top ten reasons students hate school including their commentary. This would be an excellent social studies exercise, by posting them on display and asking for student comment. If you have a lot of introverts in your classroom, perhaps show the list and ask them to comment.

The website (www.thetoptens.com/reasons-kids-hate-school) lists many reasons given, well beyond their top ten, but I found it interesting since these "issues" or gripes, will be exaggerated even more so with your at-risk students. Remember, they are labeled "at-risk", partially because they cannot attend a traditional school setting.

These are the top ten reasons listed on the above website:

1. Homework
2. Bullies
3. Getting up in the Morning
4. It's Just Boring

5. Grades
6. Annoying People
7. Physical Education
8. Exams
9. Bitchy Popular Girls
10. School Lunch

The website goes on with, last count, over 100 reasons given by students, but some overlap and refer to similar complaints. After twenty years of teaching, I have heard these complaints in one form or another. But from the viewpoint of an "at-risk" student, these complaints, justify why they are "at-risk" and placed in Alternative Education.

Before I address each one, I would like to again explain how I would use this list either the first or second day of class. Since we can see from the list, that many students "hate" school, you can have your students agree or disagree or amend these complaints, and then, either as a group or individually, have them compile, how THEY, as teachers, would correct these issues.

Lets' take the complaint of **homework**. When I was in school, it seemed as if each teacher felt obligated to give at least one hour of homework for their class. Being the "best practice" at the time, our parents expected us to do so when we got home. In my case, no television or fun stuff until the homework was completed.

In an alternative education environment, I have found that nearly all my students disliked homework.

Their rationale was that for almost 8 hours, they were stuck in school, doing school work, and now, after putting up with that, they did not feel that they needed to bring this home with them. Since I worked my students from start to end of class, I rarely issued homework other than a term project, research paper or something to do with a sporting event, feature film, political debate, or some type of competition (more on that later).

In a lock-down facility, such as juvenile hall, it was almost impossible to issue homework since the students did not have access to computers after the teaching staff left, nor could they have books in their cells. For me, that was just another explanation I used to convince my students why I worked them so hard during our 8 AM - 2 PM time frame.

However, I would take them on when they started to complain about traditional schools making them do homework with the analogy of some adults (maybe their parents) having to take work home, to impress the boss, perhaps even to keep their job. Some students agreed with this being a requirement, but most would make a smartass comment about how they would quit that job. Remember, most of your "at-risk" students do now have great role models.

You will have to work with your district regarding how they feel about issuing homework assignments, but if you are questioned about your philosophy, you can state that you work your students hard from the beginning of the school day to the end, and therefore, except for rare occasions, opt out of issuing homework. You can then tell your "at-risk" students, that you stood up for them about having to do homework, but it all depends on if they do the work you assign during the school day.

Bullying – is never tolerated in my classroom, and you must constantly be on guard for it. It may seem harmless at the start, by someone calling another student "gay," or "faggot." "dumbass," "stupid," or God forbid the "N" word, could result in a fight in your classroom. You must stop it immediately. Most districts have established policies on how to deal with bullying as well as cyberbullying.

I would ask my students if they were ever told the phrase, "Stick and stones may break my bones, but words will never harm me." Most of your students will finish the phrase before you do, indicating that they have heard it before. Ask your students what the phrase means. After you get some answers, give them your take: that it means we should not go out an assault someone just because they said something we do not like. In other words, don't be "thin skinned."

Assuming you get buy-in from what you said, now, you put another spin on it, by saying that the phrase is wrong if taken literally. By that you mean, "Bones can be repaired, but a person's feelings are very, very hard to repair," leading into discussions about how someone they may have heard of, committed suicide because of name calling or bullying. It could open-up talks about Columbine, or the mass shooting inside the theater in Aurora, Colorado.

The more you can relate classroom exercises and work to real life situations, the more your students will participate and see the relevance of why they are doing the work.

Getting Up in the Morning – another complaint I heard a lot or witnessed in my classrooms, with students putting their heads down on the desktop and falling asleep. There is a lot of current research that perhaps, due to the formation of the adolescent brain, maybe the school day should start later. Maybe, but as teachers, our assignments dictate when to be in the classroom, the bell schedule and unless the board of education for your district changes the school hours, you and your students must deal with it.

Even humans have different activity levels throughout a day. For me, I am an early bird. While teaching my at-risk student in our newly created military style boot-camp academy, I got up at 4 AM and was at school by 5 AM, writing the notes for the classes on an old fashion chalkboard. I had several students that arrived at 5:30 AM to have breakfast with me while I instructed them in Algebra.

At the same time, I had students that were chronically late and faced losing merits due to their actions (or inactions). Their parents, when contacted, would also offer an excuse such as, "Well, he doesn't sleep well at night." Most of the time I suspected that these students "do not sleep well at night," because they were out partying with their friends, getting drunk or high, or playing video games into the wee hours of the morning of a school day.

To handle this, I asked the students, what type of career they wanted. Thankfully, they did not say they wanted a job on the graveyard shift somewhere. Typically, they had visions of an 8-5 job, with weekends and holidays off. So, I had them put themselves in the place of their future supervisor and asked them, what they would do to their employee who consistently came in late. They got the point.

Believe me, it works. One of my students that I nicknamed "Sleepy," graduated and enlisted in the Army where he became a tank driver. When I first heard that he was going into the Army, I joked with him that I hoped the Army did not give him a tank, since he would fall asleep and forget where he parked it.

It's Just So Boring – Initially on day one, I explained to my students what courses we will be covering. In my alternative education setting both in juvenile hall and later, while I ran the Alder Grove Academy, we were expected to include all the curriculum needed by our students even during their incarceration. This could be a problem, since in juvenile hall, due to its lockdown status, you will have a set number of students who not only may be at different grade levels, but also at different academic levels.

Gary J. Rose, Ph.D.

For example, when assigned to our county's juvenile hall, I was given what was called the A-unit pod. Due to my former law enforcement background (since these were the older, more sophisticated males of the institution), both my supervisor and he probation administration felt it was a good fit. For many, this was not the first time they had been arrested and confined to the juvenile detention facility. Some were gang members or what we call "want-a-bees." Their crimes range from drug possession, under the influence, theft, burglary, robbery, assault, battery, gang affiliation, arson, and violation of probation.

Initially, the juvenile detention facility had three pods labeled A, B, and C. There was also a Maximum-security unit located a distance from the three general housing pods (A-C) and separated by several doors. A-unit as I stated before was for the older males. B-Unit was for the older females, and C-Unit was for the younger male and females. The Max unit housed those juveniles being charged with major offenses such as sexual assault (rape) and other sexual crimes, homicide, mayhem, juveniles from the other units that created problems including fighting, sick individuals until they felt better, pregnant females, and those with major psychological problems.

The reason I have taken some time to describe which unit housed what type of offenders, is that when a teacher was assigned any of these units, not only was the student population made up of various age groups, but also various criminal offenses, grade levels, and academic abilities, not to mention the constant noise disruption of students being moved to other units, going to court, professional visits, or a student deliberately trying to disrupt the class in session.

Add to this, students being burdened not only with going to class, but being faced with the unknown regarding what was eventually going to happen to them (sentencing, out of house placement etc.), and you can see that if your teaching style and material are judged "boring," you have a lot of work cut out for you.

So how do you make it "not boring?" I personally feel that most students at the elementary and high school level today, want to learn, but they want to be entertained at the same time. If you were to ask them, and I did, what makes a good teacher, they will tell you that their favorite teacher(s) made things fun.

An assignment I made up for my classes, asked them to write an essay on what makes a good teacher, and conversely, what makes a bad teacher. They were then asked to describe their favorite teacher from the past and why they like that individual. I sincerely wanted their input, but at the same time I got them writing, which for some, is like pulling teeth. I then listed their comments on the whiteboard, or chalkboard, depending on my classroom, those qualities they gave regarding a good teacher. I followed this up with their views of the qualities of a bad teacher. We got into a lot of great debates, and I found that even my introverts got involved. The "experts" call this engagement. I just call it good teaching.

Gary J. Rose, Ph.D.

Getting back to the "it's boring" complaint, my advice for you is to think of those teachers you had in the past, that you really liked. Why did you like him/her? Then, look at your prepared lesson plan. Is it boring and if so, can you make less boring? Can you add some jokes? Can you use some of your non-shy students in scenarios to get your students to laugh? Can you make the lesson plan applicable to real life situations? This leads to life-skill training.

I will offer some of the lesson plans I used over the years and how I got my whole class "engaged" and excited about the topic at hand. Even math can be made fun. You should research how other "excellent" teachers got their awards from their prior students, where they were judged as "their favorite" teacher.

I hated attending staff meetings and especially professional development. I would much rather be in the classroom than listen to a bunch of new, state of the art, teaching methods, being pushed by some think tank or consultant group which I knew I would never use. I wish instead that our alternative education department, would have invited teachers that would share exciting ideas that they utilized in their classrooms, that made them inspirational teachers.

For example, Jaime Escalante was very inspirational to me after I had read his book and later, viewed the movie *Stand and Deliver*. If you have never seen the movie, I highly recommend it. In fact, I continue to use this film as an inspiration for my adult inmates, but I digress. In the film, Escalante presents an Algebra problem to his students. The problem is about a boy who has a lot of girlfriends. One of the students says to Escalante, that it does not make sense since he could not see its relevance in the real world. Even with Mr. Escalante's two supervisors monitoring his teaching in the room, he quickly asked both, if they could get a few gigolos so that he could illustrate the solving of the problem. All the students laughed and his supervisors could see that he had all his students engaged.

In another scene, he is introducing them to the difference between positive and negative numbers. How does he do this so that his students could visualize the concept? He asked how many of them had ever gone to the beach? He got a show of hands. Then he asked them if they ever played in the sand? Again, almost everyone raised their hands. Knowing that they now had this visual in their minds, he uses his hand to dig out some sand. He tells his class that the sand in his hand represents a positive number. The hole is the negative number. On the board, he had a simple equation of $+1 + -1 =?$ He asked one of his gangbangers what the answer was, saying, "fill the hold." The gangbanger realized that if you took one handful of sand out of the ground, you would need to put one handful of sand back to fill the hole, leaving you nothing, or zero.

Escalante referred to a real-life situation; playing with sand at the beach. Many of my successful lesson plans where made relevant to my students. You will find, that the more relevant, the more real life situation in which you can demonstrate to your students regarding your lesson plan, the more successful you will be.

Grades – there are some "experts" out there who want to eliminate the issuance of grades, feeling that it makes it too stressful for students. I totally disagree, but like many things I taught in my classrooms, you must get "buy-in" from your students. Again, you must show them the relevance.

Another teacher that I found inspirational, who began teaching just prior to me, used one of the same techniques I used in my classrooms, related to grades. LouAnne Johnson, who was portrayed in the film *Dangerous Minds,* told her students that at that moment, each of them had an A in English. Some of the actors playing the part of her students, could not believe this since they had never earned an A before. Whether this occurred or not in real-life, you will have to ask Ms. Johnson, but what I found powerful in this segment of the film, was that students valued earning an A. She got their attention.

While assigned to juvenile hall, we did not issue letter grades. Due to the transient nature of our students, you could not justifiably award them a letter grade since they were not with you long enough. Instead, they received a pass/fail check in their file and were given the amount of credit earned in the appropriate courses taught per hours of instruction. For example, if a student was in my class for thirty days studying Algebra, he would receive a pass/fail for 30 hours of Algebra credit, providing he passed the tests I gave to him.

At the Alder Grove Academy, I decided that I needed a campus-wide grading system that not only I would follow, but also the teacher initially assigned to our seventh and eighth graders. I am glad I adopted this grading system, since, due to budget cuts, the second teacher was re-assigned and I now had a classroom of 42 students from grades $7^{th} - 12^{th}$. Grading was done on a straight percentage basis.

$$100\% - 90\% = A$$
$$89\% - 80\% = B$$
$$79\% - 70\% = C$$
$$69\% - 60\% = D$$
$$59\% - 0\% = Hello!!!!!!$$

I got buy-in from my students by asking for volunteers to see if they would share their ultimate career choice. They had no idea what I was up too, which I liked. I would share with them the projected salary they would earn if they took the necessary steps in their educational career to secure their desired job. In doing so, I reviewed their pathways to their future careers. Their answers ran the gamete; veterinary assistant, welder, chef, lawyer, dental assistant, carpenter, painter, plumber, hairdresser. Each one they selected would result in my placing an approximate hourly or yearly salary for that job.

Gary J. Rose, Ph.D.

I will state that I am an educator who does not believe that every student should go to college. Making that a "political dream" by our elected officials, is unrealistic. Some individuals do well in college, but others, who truly want to be a house painter, mechanic, welder or other manual laborer, should be encouraged to pursue their dream and not be forced to take courses to get into the university system just because some legislator somewhere wants to brag that all the kids in his/her district, are preparing to enter college.

Returning to grades, I would then explain to them, that when they get their dream jobs, what do they expect to receive at the end of the work week. Of course, I anticipated their responses and hoped that they would say, a paycheck. Once I get that out of them, I tell them that grades are like that paycheck they expect for their work. Then I asked them, "If they failed to do a good job at work, what might happen?" Their answers will range for a loss of wages, to termination.

Grades, I explain, is a way that both they and I can use to judge how well they are doing their work. A student that does *A* work, deserves an *A* grade. A student that does *B* work, deserves a *B* grade and so one. Of course, a student that does *F* work cannot get fired from class, like he/she would if they did poorly on the job, but they will need to turn their production around so that they can pass high school or move from junior high to high school. Again, do this to get their buy-in.

I then handed out a composition book or lab book. I have them place their names on the front of the binder. I issued them a ruler, and I have them make columns for each subject taught each day. At the academy, that included Algebra (pre-Algebra), Science, U.S. History, World History, U.S. Government, Economics, English, and P/E. Eight courses, eight columns. I would have them put a date for today, and then tell them to place a letter grade A in each column. You will get a lot of at-risk students looking at you, to which I would joke, "gee, Doctor Rose, what have you been smoking?"

I would follow my joke with the truth, I never have smoked since I have asthma. Why share that with my students? For me, although this is personal, it shows my students that I am human. I might be their teacher and represent authority, but I am still human. Amazingly, I get students who later, tell me that they are also asthmatic or have other physical problems, and thank me for sharing. This is up to you. You do not have to do this.

After they fill-in their columns with an *A* grade, I make sure that they listed today's date. Then I explain the following, "*As of today, each of you has an A in all of those courses. You will find that it is easier to earn an A than it is to keep it. Each Friday is Pay Day; our weekly test. I will try to grade everyone's exam before school is out so that you can put your new weekly grades in your binder. Your parents have been told that at any time, they can ask you or me, what your current grades are as well as your grade point average.*

That's it. That is how simple it is to convince them how important their grades are. I never graded on a curve. My students were told that they were not competing with any other student. It was them against me. I even wore a black shirt on Fridays (Payday) that had a saying from then San Francisco 49ers coach Mike Singleterry, which read, *"Don't tell me, show me."* I told my students that on Fridays, "don't tell me how smart you are, show me." This was my challenge to them and most of the students loved it.

Remember, many of your at-risk students have cut school, have tardiness or attendance problems, and some have never had to be accountable for their actions due to poor parenting. But, if you take the time and show them that they are not failures by awarding them a decent grade, you will start to see a sparkle in their eyes. But they must earn it.

I did not encourage grade inflation which sadly, some teachers and administrators seem to relish. I feel that this sets up students for failure down the road. Here is an example. I had a student incarcerated in juvenile hall who was unable to perform most basic math problems, yet he told me he did not need math since he had already earned his Algebra credits. I had my teaching assistant check for me so that when I challenged him, I would have his records, showing that he lied to me. Instead, to my surprise, there it was, (5) credits in Algebra, earning a grade of C.

I still decided to challenge him by giving him a simple equation of $2x + x = 12$. He had no clue regarding its solution but instead, asked if he could talk to me privately. We walked into a room used for book storage and he informed me that, while attending a continuation high school, his teacher made him a deal. If he would play video games in the back of the classroom and not disrupt the class during Algebra, he would give him a passing grade of *C*. Now this same student was faced with the California High School Exit Exam, which, at the time, was a requirement in California to graduate from high school. He was not prepared for this examination, especially in math, meaning that his likelihood of passing the exam was slim. He never did pass that exam and thus, did not earn his high school diploma. I lost track of this student and pray to God that he did not end up in prison, but somehow found a rewarding job and is doing well.

Many professors in our colleges and universities are noticing a rise in new freshmen students with outstanding high school grades, having to take remedial courses in math and English, since they are not prepared for the rigors of college level instruction. I feel it goes back to grade inflation by some teachers and less than challenging curriculums.

As a side note, at the Alder Grove Academy, each student, called a cadet, reported to a sergeant of their platoon. That sergeant had the added responsibility of monitoring his/her cadets' grades. The sergeant could come to me and request another cadet for another platoon, to help the struggling cadet in whatever course was needed. Later, with the help of army personnel, we assigned what we called, "Battle Buddies" at the beginning of each semester, who teamed with each cadet helping them in whatever course they were struggling. I would match up a student good in math, with a student who needed help. The student who provided the mentoring got an award. More on that later.

Annoying People/Bitchy Popular Girls – This happens in every class I had, including my current students, incarcerated adults. You and I have been in situations where someone just annoys us, but, since we had good role models (parents), we know how to tolerate these situations without it becoming a verbal or physical altercation. Not so with many at-risk students who did not receive that mentorship. To them, the annoying person must be called out and dealt with. The same goes with some girls being upset with popular girls in the classroom. God, help you if they suspect that this popular girl is hitting on their boyfriend.

In the Academy one morning right after I just arrived, I found a phone message from my supervisor, telling me that she had received a phone call from a parent of one of my female cadets, who informed her of a fight that took place the night before. She wanted me give me a heads-up in case it carried over that morning. Before the students arrived, I was able to reached her and was informed that a group of my female and male cadets, had "shoulder-tapped" a person going into a liquor store, and who got them some alcohol. While drinking, a male and female cadet when off together being observed by the male's girlfriend. When they returned, it was learned by the group that the two had had sex. Accusations flew and a brawl broke out, only breaking up when they heard sirens approaching.

"Great," I told her. I have a full agenda of classwork to do, and dealing with a bunch of female's drama would take over the whole morning. Thank God, my supervisor said that she would be coming over and would talk with the girls. Even behind a closed door and down from the main classroom, we could all hear the "bitch, whore, slut" accusations fly. I am not sure how my supervisor was able to calm them down, but after about 90 minutes, they all returned to class and there were no more fights between them.

My only intervention was to welcome them back to class and tell them to get notes from another cadet because they had a big exam on Friday. Note: the more work you can give to your students throughout the school day, the less chance they have for going astray. With at-risk students, if you have any time where there is nothing structurally for them to do, they will take advantage of that time and you will spend energy getting the class focused again.

Fortunately, in the Academy, there really was no distinction between males and females regarding dress. To eliminate gang members (and yes, I had rival gang members in the Academy) from wearing their "colors," they all wore cameo flag uniforms like that worn by the Army personnel working in partnership with me. The females shared that initially they hated the idea of wearing uniforms, but then liked the idea since, in the morning, they only had to worry about makeup. Later, during Social Studies and life skills, they realized that many of the other students in their class, came from poor families and they were embarrassed while attending their traditional schools because they wore hand-me-downs and not modern clothing. Many of those students refused to go to school to avoid ridicule.

Exams – Ask your students, why educators feel a need for an exam. By doing so you are once again getting their buy-in. Once I solicited good answers, I add on my own take on the subject by using the driver's test as my example. Most of my students could not wait to get behind a wheel of their own car. I asked them how they earn the right to drive. They answered, "By taking a written and behind the wheel exam." I ask why? They look at me quizzically, but then understand where I am coming from. "You have to prove to the State of California, in both a written and driving test, that you can drive a car." That is an exam.

"In education, your "driver's exam" with me, is our weekly test. I need to know that you understand the topic and I can either do so with a verbal exam, an essay exam or a combination, like our exam on "Payday," I added.

While on the subject, I told them the following: *As a teacher, I am always amazed after I score an exam, by hearing students say, "hey, I got a B, or hey, I got an A." Then I hear a student complain, "Mr. Rose hates me, he gave me a D."* What is wrong with this logic I ask?

My point is that in each incident, the student EARNED the grade they received. I did not just give it to them out of thin air. I then said, *"The student that said he got an A, earned that A grade. Therefore, the student who got that D grade* (they would finish my sentence for me) *earned the D grade."*

Physical Education and School Lunch – Is it surprising to learn about the obesity problem in our schools? It shouldn't be. We are a nation addicted to the convenience of fast food, even with phrases such as "supersize me." Yet, in many of our schools, physical education has been eliminated or minimized to the extent that it is not surprising that we have kids as young as five years old suffering from obesity and diabetes.

Our former first lady, Michelle Obama thought that the answer was a more wholesome school lunch which resulted in more food being thrown away after lunch and more students going without anything to eat until they got home. And once they get home, what do they do? They grab a sugar drink, high-fat snacks, lay on their bed or couch, and play video games, text, watch television or listen to music.

Admitting that I am getting old, I remember how much I looked forward to P.E. in both elementary, junior high and high school. I joked about how P/E and lunch were my favorite subjects. When I got home from school, the rule was homework first, before I could go out and play with my friends. We loved to play baseball and football until it got dark and we had to head home. In high school, not only did we have P.E. during the normal school day, but we had high school sports; football, baseball, tennis, golf, cross country, track, swimming, and basketball.

Part of the problem I feel is that some in our society feel that competition is bad. They feel that there should not be winners and losers and that everyone should get the same award for "participating." My sister recently told me that after relocating in the state of Colorado, she and my brother-in-law attended their grandson's first Little League game and learned that not only is the score not taken or posted, but parents are reminded not to cheer even when their son or daughter they came to see play, does something good. How that is supposed to set them up to handling failures they will personally face when they are adults, I do not understand.

If you teach in a traditional school, you probably do not have much input about the physical education of your students, nor what is being served in the cafeteria. I was fortunate to have my own school in three different locations. Since many of my students were expelled and/or court/probation referred, they had to be a certain distance away from traditional schools.

Except for one of the sites, we could use the surrounding areas as our physical education field. Working with at-risk students, I have learned that they need the ability to get some fresh air and exercise to stay focused on my curriculum. But there always was a caveat; they had to earn it. That's correct. Unless they completed the work assigned, followed the classroom's rules (more on that later) and worked as a team, they would forfeit the period I set aside for physical education. This really works well in getting your class to feel that they are all in it together. They start pulling for each other, all to save their "sacred" physical education time together. You are again teaching them life skills.

I did not count mini-breaks as part to their physical education time. I would call them "potty" breaks and they were normally five minutes in length. Here is a look at our typical agenda which was always displayed on either the chalkboard or whiteboard, before my students arrived:

0800-0805 Coffee, donut (on Paydays only), hot chocolate, attendance taking
0805-0900 Algebra, general math
0900-0955 Science (General, Life Science, Earth Science) Marine Biology
0955-1000 Break time
1000-1055 English (Literature, essay writing, creative writing, grammar)

1055-1150 Physical education
1150-1230 Lunch
1230-1330 World History, U.S. History, Geography, U.S. Government
1330-1430 Wrap up (continued with history), electives, economics, art, projects.

Since I worked my students hard Monday – Thursday, Friday was more of a kickback day following their 2-3-hour comprehensive examination. As stated before, I called it Payday – Don't Tell Me, Show Me.

I would bring in whatever number of donuts I needed, depending on the class size. By the time my students arrived, I would have a large coffee pot made as well as another coffee pot dedicated to hot water. The students who wanted hot chocolate fended for themselves. Some were entrepreneurs, and went to a thrift grocery store, and brought in several additional servings of powder hot chocolate mix, and sold them to their classmates. Others loved making Top Ramen for breakfast in addition to their donut.

Treating them as adults, I allowed them to eat and drink whatever they had on their desk, if they worked on their exam. Their exam was comprised of all the lessons we covered during the week. Therefore, they had Algebra, Science, U.S. History, World History, English and an elective topic, each containing at least 10-15 questions. There were always at least sixty questions for them to solve/answer. By "setting them up," no one ever complained about the length of these exams. There were several students over the years, that would comment before the exam, "Bring it on Mr. Rose," indicating that they accepted my challenge.

After they completed their exam, I allowed them to socialize and work on whatever they wanted to do until the rest of their classmates finished. If, however, they began making too much noise, they knew I had "my" material that they could work on: normally more Algebra or math problems.

To celebrate their efforts during the week, I would bring in a movie and we would finish Friday viewing a film, and occasionally, my top students would make popcorn in the popcorn machine I had purchased for the class. While the students watched the film, I would grade their exams and post on the top of each section, their score. Therefore, at the end of each week, my students had a weekly score in Algebra, Science, English, U.S./World History, U.S. Government, P/E, and an elective. In the academy, each cadet was to enter this information into their binder and show it to their sergeant who would note any grades lower than a C. Most of the videos/DVDs I used dealt with true stories to help build their life skills.

Did everyone like physical education? The answer is no. Some had such poor self-esteem issues about their athletic abilities that they did not want to embarrass themselves. Others were so obese that they did not want to participate, knowing in advance, that they could not keep up with their classmates. Some frankly were lazy and tried to refuse to do anything.

Gary J. Rose, Ph.D.

While assigned to our juvenile detention facility, one of the first things I did away with was allowing students to lay on the floor with blankets. Probation made that request on my first day of teaching. I thought that they were teasing me since most of them knew my background in law enforcement and knew my brother, who, as a lieutenant with the local sheriff's department, taught them weaponless defense. I laughed and said, "No one will be sleeping in my classroom." Then I realized that they were not joking.

Since I was just starting out as a new teacher, I decided that I would post daily, the classroom assignments. Sandwiched in the agenda was physical education with a question mark next to it. The students would file into the classroom from their upstairs or downstairs cells. At least one student would ask what the question mark stood for next to P/E. I told them that "they" had to earn it. This was something new to them. In the past, they automatically assumed, that they got physical education. Some would play basketball, some would walk, and some would lay on the concrete and sleep.

By setting my agenda up this way, physical education was a reward that they had to earn. They got their large muscle movement in walking to and from the cafeteria for breakfast, lunch and dinner, so probation's responsibility to make sure each student had a period in which these muscles were addressed, was satisfied. In addition, after school was out, the probation officers assigned to each unit, brought them out for one hour of exercise. Therefore, no one would complain about not getting enough exercise during the week, but boy would they get upset when they lost the right to P/E.

Physical education was presented in a fun way at the juvenile detention facility. I bought a lot of plastic baseballs with holes in them. I would tape them up using duct tape and then poke holes through the tape into the holes of the balls with my pen. This allowed air to still pass through the baseballs and the tape gave them some weight for pitching and added strength.

Regulation sized plastic bats were also taped up with the all reliable duct tape to give them some extra weight. Teams were formed in the classroom with the caveat that everyone played, or we would not go out. Yes, that is called peer pressure. Believe me, they will get over it and start playing as a team. Everyone in the pod (A-unit) already knew who the best players were. By making them team captains, the talent was divided from the start. Teams were picked and then I had the captains call it while I flipped a coin to see who batted first.

It wasn't just about going out and playing baseball. It was what the experts call a teaching moment in which I talked about sportsmanship, teamwork, strategies, helping a fellow team member who may not be as skilled as they were. A probation officer or I did the pitching since there was always the chance of one student taking it out on another by hitting them with a pitch on purpose.

Gary J. Rose, Ph.D.

The other sports we played inside the indoor courtyard area, which was a large concrete area with three-quarters covered by the roof, and one quarter open with heavy duty cyclone fencing covering that space; was volleyball, basketball, and for a long time, arena football.

The probation department spray painted bases on the floor as well as the home plate. The rules, like Major League Baseball, were followed for the most part. Three strikes you were out. Four balls and you walked. Hit by a pitch gave you first base etc. Now, where they changed: It a batter hit any portion of the ceiling, you were automatically out. The ceiling had some fire retardant sprayed on metal beams, and even though we played with plastic balls and bats, my students generated a lot of bat speed while hitting, and several times a large section of "ceiling" would fall. If a foul ball with the side walls and was caught before hitting the ground, you were out. Sometimes I allowed stealing of bases. There was a catcher, 1st baseman and, depending on how a team wanted to defend, other bases or a lot of outfielders. The first team to reach 15 runs over the other team, won. You got it – the slaughter rule.

Volleyball could be played several different ways; traditional, Olympic, or what I called, ghetto ball. If given a choice, they all wanted to play ghetto ball. The rules were simple, there weren't many. There was no rotation of severs. Whoever they selected to serve when they had the ball, could do so. Each side could hit the volleyball three times per side. Therefore, a weak sever could hit the ball to one of his teammates, who could hit it up and down twice before having to send it over the net. You could not pull on the net, but you could crash into it. In other words, unless I saw you deliberately pull on the net, hitting it with your hands was ok. Serving the ball off the wall which would normally be out of bounds, was ok, if the ball hit back into the court.

Why such weird rules? Because it required a lot of teamwork to strategize how to defend and attack the other team. Probation loved it since the students really got into the whole competition thing and were exhausted after one hour of play. When we got back into the classroom and the rehydrated, they were extremely focused for the rest of my curriculum.

Basketball was the hardest sport to referee since the good ballers all thought that they never created a foul. I also had to contend with the ball hogs who refused to spread the ball around. Another problem with basketball was that in juvenile hall, the basketball court was far from regulation and to put 10 at-risk students on the court banging into each other, caused more concern than it was worth.

Arena football was great while it lasted. Yes, we had at-risk students pick teams and play flag football indoors. There were very few rules. Everyone was eligible to run, throw or go out for a pass. You could not rush the quarterback unless he decided to run. Sometimes I allowed rushing the quarterback after counting out loud to five. The field of play was the same rectangle concrete perimeter we used for baseball and basketball.

For years, we never had any injuries playing arena football. I could not say the same with volleyball and outdoor football. In volleyball, we had several players dislocate their knees or jamb their fingers. In outdoor football, we had hamstring injuries, dislocated fingers, dislocated knees, scrapes and scratches, and poked eyes. Our main concern playing outdoor football was that we combined my older male wards, with the older female wards. We had to watch for illegal "grabbing," usually loved by the females!

Arena football ended after a student got injured and broke his arm. He was a student you will run into, who walks around like a zombie and is proud of it. If you look up lackadaisical, you would see a picture of him. He seemed to relish on getting his fellow students upset with his lack of performance. He just had an "I don't care attitude" and his own team did not hesitate in showing their disdain for him. One day it happened. The probation staff and I were busy watching the play go downfield and then saw the student on the ground withering in pain, while grabbing his arm.

Apparently, there was some collusion between the two teams in which the offensive team deliberately did not block pass rushers who "bull" rushed over the injured player. He was not paying attention and down he went. Physical education for the day was over and so was arena football.

In the Alder Grove Academy, I had 7th – 12th grade males and females, including rival gang members. I had tremendous athletes, both males and females, non-athletic types, and flat lazy types. Most, if not all however, were type A personality, all wanting to be the alpha male or female.

Before our P/E period, I lectured them on sportsmanship, leadership and how the real world is competitive. I would also have a prepared presentation on obesity, heart disease, diabetes etc. My intention was to scare the hell out of them about the sedentary lifestyle some of them were living. I showed them slides of plaque building up in arteries and pictures of children posted on the Internet that were grossly obese. That got their attention.

To motivate them, I showed them the movie *Rudy* and discussed individuals who put their size and athletic ability aside and still competed against those more athletic. Once I had the class convinced that it was not how good you were, it was that you helped your team, they competed against each other.

My females were as aggressive in sports as my males, especially when playing flag football. I installed a rule in which every other play, had to include the use of a female. She could not just hike the ball or block. She had to be utilized as a quarterback, runner, or pass receiver. These really got both the guys and girls working together. No longer could one or two males dominate the game. It was impressive to see how many guys protected their female teammates.

Gary J. Rose, Ph.D.

My army co-instructors always stressed teamwork and when they conducted physical training, a lot of the exercises were team inspired. From tug-a-war to running drills, the platoons had to work together. Even during Ranger runs, the entire class had to work as a team. Prima donnas hurt the entire class but soon, they become conformers. They not only became a team, but later, referred to the academy as their home and fellow classmates and teaching staff, like family.

Some of you might consider some of the activities I used as risky and you are correct. From arena football to ghetto volleyball, there was always the risk that someone might get hurt, and some did. My students realized that some of the sports we participated in could result in injury and they watched out for each other and knew, that if I saw any unsportsmanlike activity or out and out retaliation, not only was P/E over for the day, but they faced suspension from me.

My female students, especially when it was raining, loved to have earned the right after participating in flag football, to play "fumble drills." I would pick the wettest part of the field and have my ladies who wanted to participate, stand in front of me, facing straight ahead. Then, without warning, I would throw a football into an area of the field and shout "fumble." The object was for them to race to the ball, field it, and bring it back to me. While running to the ball, they could knock down or tackle their opposition. Sometimes I allowed them to pick a partner to help them get the ball and make it back to my position. They loved it and were very disappointed on those days that I said we would not be having fumble drills. Normally it was due to the class getting me upset and I let them know that they lost the chance to tackle each other.

The real world involves competition. Allowing your students to experience both winning and losing, is important for them in adulthood. Lecture your students about how some very successful individuals had to overcome obstacles, setbacks, and other forms of "losing," before they succeeded.

Sadly, some of our millennials, raised or educated in systems that do not stress winning and losing or competition, do not have the ability to handle failure. They seemed to believe that simply showing up with a college degree, means that they should make a six-figure salary and not have to perform. Just showing up for work, in their world, is enough to justify their salary and benefits. They do not believe that they must be accountable for their actions. They have always received "awards" just for participating, so why should work be any different?

"If you can't figure out your purpose, figure out your passion. Your passion will lead you right into your purpose."

—Bishop T.D. Jakes

TEACHER TRAINING PROGRAMS AND AT-RISK STUDENTS

America's schools are beset by the problem of disruptive and violent behaviors. In a 2006 poll, respondents rated fighting, violence and gangs as the most pressing problems facing their public schools and pointed to lack of discipline as a significant secondary problem (Rose & Gallup, 2006). A nationwide survey of teachers, students and police at the same time, found that all constituencies believed schools were being compromised by disruptive and aggressive behaviors and classroom violence (Finn, Finn, & Scott, 2008). Yet teachers rarely receive the training they need in classroom management and de-escalation of violence (Todras, 2007). As any police officer on the beat will attest, on-the-job conflict management skills are extraordinarily valuable; however, in her detailed phenomenological study of ex-service members who become teachers, Todras (2007) found that many teachers desire better, more forthright training. Moreover, schools are chronically underfunded and short staffed, particularly in urban areas. There are too many demands facing teachers and schools, which can cause cohesive classroom management training to be given a low priority.

There have been many initiatives conducted by authorities, such as the establishment of school safety committees and the Positive Behavior Intervention Supports (PBIS) program, which I will discuss later. These initiatives are geared towards empowering school communities and keeping both students and teachers safe. However, devising a training plan that empowers teachers to face the real- life difficulties in our present-day classrooms like that followed by police officers, who are adequately trained to face the real-life experiences in our societies, may take some of the pressure off our teachers, and help them to be more effective in teaching their classroom lessons and enable our schools to improve (Bernstein, 2006).

Every teacher must be able to teach effectively every time they teach a lesson to their students and, consequently, improve the performance of the schools. The effectiveness of the teachers in managing student behavior, which is often overlooked, is really the most important factor in the educational sector (Bernstein, 2006).

Some research studies have revealed that most pre-service teachers, fresh from colleges and entering the teaching profession, come into the classrooms with much enthusiasm, zeal and drive to make a difference and bring a positive change to the lives of any class of students they are assigned to teach (MetLife, Inc., 2011). These pre-service teachers attend colleges or universities and will graduate with their respected four year degrees and normally, one additional year of teacher training (Robers, Zhang, & Truman, 2012).

Depending on their states' teacher licensing procedures, most will be mandated to attend what is commonly referred to as the teacher college. These institutions are responsible for introducing these new teachers into the science of education; covering many areas including subject mastery, as demonstrated in various state- mandated examinations. In addition, in the State of California, they must also pass a Reading Instruction Competence Assessment (RICA); pass or take a semester course regarding the U.S. Constitution, Computer Technology, Educational Foundations and Instruction in Language Arts (Robers, Zhang, & Truman, 2012).

Upon graduating from their teacher colleges, if hired, the new teacher is assigned to their first classroom. It is there that the theoretical aspects of their individual subject areas, students and classrooms they had studied with their professors while in their teacher colleges, collide with real-world classroom behavioral issues. Unfortunately, these pre-service teachers soon discover that they have not been well prepared to deal with the increase in violence, disruptive behavior, and disrespect they are exposed to in their K-12 classrooms. In fact, available statistics shows that crime rate in schools is alarming. During the school year 2009-2010, available data shows that 85% of government schools recorded the occurrence of one or more crime-related incidents within the school. By simple inference, the national estimates amount to about 1.9 million crimes which translate to a rate of 40 crimes per 1,000 students enrolled in the public schools during this period (Robers, Zhang, & Truman, 2012).

Beyond students' misbehaviors that derives from poor parenting and self-esteem, recent research reports show that a worrisome percentage, between 12- 22 percent, of students in school have issues related to a behavior disorder that could be diagnosed as either mental or emotional (Adelman & Taylor, 1988). In addition, many children and youth in the United States have been strongly linked to a chain of developmental behaviors such as child aggression, delinquency, antisocial tendencies and sometimes violence (Walker, Ramsey, & Gresham, 2004).

In 1979, an American Russian psychologist, Urie Bronfenbrenner, introduced his Socio-ecological theory and stated that an increasing number of children from at-risk backgrounds were showing what he termed "well-developed patterns of antisocial behavior" to the schooling process. Many of these children were said to have exhibited extreme deficiencies in their school- readiness skills

The reasons for the increase of intensity and frequency range from the following reasons: abusive parents; poor parental background; deterioration of family values; inability of elders to influence the youngsters; effects of psychological disorders such as reactive attachment disorder, ADHD etc.; effects of trending culture or culture in vogue; exposure to the prevailing violence in the society; failure of the special justice system for the juvenile; poverty; access to weapons; inactivity; effects of racism; lack of ability to cope with frustration; drug abuse and effects of alcohol; video games; song lyrics; Internet; inability of societal groups of society to promote high achievement among youngsters; and lack of positive and mutual working relationships between schools and parents.

Research studies have identified school violence as the most substantial problems facing schools in the U.S. The objective of this report is to gain an understanding about the prevailing delinquency in K-12 classrooms and the role of teachers in this problem.

In their fourteenth joint annual report on school crime and student safety, the National Center for Educational Statistics (NCES), the Institute of Educational Services (IES), the U.S. Department of Education, and the Bureau of Justice Statistics (BJS) and the U.S. Department of Justice, recently reported that there were 33 cases of school-associated violent deaths from July1, 2009 through June 30, 2011. Out of the 33 cases, 25 were homicides, 5 were suicide, and 3 were the result of a legal intervention (Robers, Zhang, and Truman, 2012). Before the April 20, 1999 tragic school shootings at Columbine High School in Littleton, Colorado, took place, 25% of students had reported being the victim of violence at school, and one in eight of the students had carried some kind of firearm to school. Also, 17% of teachers, which translate to one in six, had also reported being victims of violence either within or around the schools they worked. During the 2007/2008 school year alone, about 34% of teachers admitted that the misbehavior of students in class interfered with their teaching while 32% noted that class cutting and student tardiness interrupted and adversely affected the effectiveness of their class lesson (Robers, Zhang, & Truman, 2012).

Dealing with students' behavior problems is one of the most pressing concerns facing educators today and unfortunately, teachers are increasingly feeling inadequately equipped to combat the menace (Buchanan, Gueldner, Tran & Merrel, 2009; Justice & Espinoza, 2007). Indeed, all well-meaning Americans (and not just the educators) should be concerned about the state of our nation's schools because these schools need to be free of crime and violence if they are to serve as safe havens for effective teaching and learning processes. Any instances of crime and violence at school will not only affect the individuals directly concerned but also the bystanders, the educational process by way of disruption, the surrounding community and the school itself. Furthermore, when teachers get overwhelmed with too much classroom difficulties, their enthusiasm for the teaching profession wanes and their performance inevitably suffers.

Research conducted in 2008 and reported in MetLife Survey of the American Teacher (MetLife, Inc., 2011) shows that the majority of teachers really want to be more effective, and the study reported that they had shown optimism and enthusiasm for teaching prior to beginning to teach. An analysis of the survey showed that 83% of pre-service teachers agreed strongly that they could bring a positive change on the lives of their students prior to entering the profession. However, after their second year in the teaching profession, their optimism and enthusiasm began to decline (MetLife, Inc., 2011).

Prior to taking up teaching appointments, only 28% of the pre-service teachers surveyed agreed that many students came to school with so many juvenile issues that it would be difficult for them to end up being good students, but after two years on the job, the figure had gone up to 50% (MetLife, Inc., 2011).

Calls to improve school safety and discipline procedures have escalated recently, as part of a reaction to the increased attention to incidences of school violence. Schools have been doing their best to curtail misbehavior in students but it is not proving to be sufficient. For example, in a recent survey, 72% of teachers were reported to have strongly agreed or agreed that their fellow teachers at their respective schools were working to ensure school rules were strictly enforced, and a higher percentage, 89% agreed or strongly agreed that the principal enforced the school rules (MetLife, Inc., 2011).

Some measures are working but clearly more needs to be done. For example, during the school periods between 1993 and 2009, the percentage of school children who reported carrying some forms of a weapon at least once anywhere during the past 30 days declined from 22 percent to 17 percent, and the percentage who reported carrying a weapon at least one day on school property also declined from 12 percent to 6 percent. But weapons were on campuses across the United States.

(Baker, 2005) pointed out that today's educators are asked, and in many instances mandated, to meet the needs of a diverse group of students, including those with emotional and behavioral disorders. More students are culturally diverse, have English as a second language, are less prepared to enter school, and have a greater range of learning and behavior challenges. Baker (2005) also observed that for decades, educators have been examining the need to provide different classroom instruction to better meet diverse learning needs. Baker contends that such accommodations must extend beyond the academic realm and into the behavioral realm if students with emotional behavior disorders are to be provided an equal educational opportunity.

Many research studies such as the work of (Greenberg, Domitrovic, & Bumbarger, 2001) suggests that since there is no one remedy for addressing students' multidimensional disruptive behaviors, "effective strategies must consist of a broad range of strategies and sustained attention to multiple systems of intervention."

Baker (2005) ascertained that teachers who are trained to use different strategies, both instructional and disciplinary, may become ready to educate a variety of learners. Indeed, when teachers stress social skills in the classroom and create a climate of cooperation and respect for others, there are fewer discipline problems and less negative behavior (McCloud, 2005).

Teachers have one of the most important jobs to do in our society, and yet the training they receive is inconsistent at best, and at worst can be useless or even simply not exist at all. While teaching is a profession that in some cases takes years to do well, our society does not seem to feel as a whole that teachers, despite their specialized occupation, need the same sort of specialized and intensive training that other professionals receive. Putting this in medical terms highlights the problem. As parents, adults are at times leaving their children's education to people who have less training not just than their doctor, but even than the physician's assistant who makes notes or takes blood pressure. Teaching students with behavioral issues and emotional disturbances, which is increasing in mainstream (integrated) classrooms is an even greater challenge than regular teaching (Quinn, 2001) Middle schools in particular, are likely to have violent incidents, with 40 incidents per 1000 students (as opposed to 21 incidents per 1000 students in elementary and high schools) as stated in a recent United States Department of Education survey and researched by (Neiman & Hill, 2011). Since teaching middle school is difficult, these jobs where violence is more common are also more likely to go to inexperienced teachers.

In today's teacher shortage, some states have put into place alternative certification programs. Some private alternative certification programs allow students to work toward certification with extremely minimal training. If these would-be teachers can convince a principal to hire them, they are essentially thrown into the classroom with only the equivalent of a college class of training behind them. This "sink or swim" approach has been adopted by many cities that have the worst schools and problems, such as Chicago, Baltimore, and Washington DC. While some new teachers, such as those who come in with Teach for America, receive training, many others who do not have traditional backgrounds in education do not. This leads to high teacher turnover and ineffective classroom management causing frustration for both those teachers who do attempt to stick it out and for their students and administrators as well. Within the climate of the classroom, one of the greatest predictors for student academic success, are teachers who have the ability to foster a positive climate. But, unfortunately, little training in this area is given to teachers in their respective training college programs. (Sprott, 2004)

(Hirschfield & Gasper, 2011) found that students who were more engaged in school in late childhood and early adolescence, which are the crucial middle school years mentioned above, were less likely to be delinquent and engage in crime. So, teachers must be taught to engage students especially those that are displaying pre-delinquent or delinquent behavior. This again is lacking in their pre-service training. To understand the kind of training teachers, need, it is crucial to fully understand the current state of teacher training, especially as it relates to skills teachers might be able to use in a new and improved training model with elements of police training being included.

Career Development Training for Pre-Service Teachers

Historically, Zeichner (1999) discussed several models of teacher training that have been utilized within the last decades of scholarship. One model was to basically prompt teachers to show desired behaviors, which were those correlated with student learning. Teachers were given prompts to mimic and did little self-reflection, displaying desired behaviors but not necessarily taking ownership of the training material.

There are several teacher education programs Zeichner cites that are effectively preparing teachers to successfully work with diverse learners, including the economically disadvantaged and minority students that tend to populate the worst schools. Unfortunately, the emphasis is primarily in subject mastery, since it is necessary to have a grasp of their material. However, once they get to their school placement, they often find that knowing the subject is not enough. Some teachers are assigned student teaching placement to learn how to teach but with little classroom instruction other than theoretical basis (Solomon, 1987). Since much of this training is theoretical, there is no room for practical application in the pre-service curriculum dealing with unruly, disrespectful, and disorderly youth. Solomon concludes that the ideal program would combine elements of both extremes.

(Cajkler & Hall, 2009) found that new teachers are taught in the mastery their subjects, but are not taught some of the most important things that could help them succeed in difficult classrooms. One of these is how to deal with new arrivals who speak little or no English-those students who can inadvertently disrupt even the best well-run classroom. (Sternstein, 1999) addresses one way that such concerns, which are not always covered in traditional teacher training, can be addressed: a teacher- training academy for pre-service teachers that is run by current and former teachers who have experience in the same kind of urban and troubled schools that the teachers it prepares will try to enter. These "real-world" programs are often combined with student teaching experience, per (Anderson &

Stillman, 2013). However, many of these student teaching programs are not positive. The authors point out, that there is limited research as to whether or not these programs influence actual teaching practice, and they may instead contribute to reductive views of student's culture and social contexts.

(Hart & Murphy, 1990) find that teachers react to their training in different ways, depending on their intelligence level. Teachers who are more gifted academically, their interviews found, (as measured by GPA and other factors) may have more of a problem adjusting to existing structures of their training and first year teaching. These especially gifted potential teachers are often frustrated that teacher education, both in pre-service through their second year, does not adequately prepare them for the realities of their jobs. As a result, these teachers leave the profession in disproportionately high numbers.

(Denscombe, 1982) believes that pre-service teaching programs focus too little on building a community of these new and aspiring teachers. While they may have many of the same hopes, dreams, and fears, existing teaching training programs tend to focus on classroom control, but not effectively. This has the effect of making these new teachers feel that they are failing, close the doors to their classrooms, teach in isolation, and believe that this is what they are supposed to be doing. New teachers, whatever their specific training, are loath to ask for help, and therefore often end up extremely lonely and isolated within their first year, again leading to high teacher turnover.

Clearly, what is being done now is not working. (Starr, 2012) characterizes his pre-service teaching experience in a negative way, citing a lack of depth and a huge gap between what training says are best practices and what goes on in the classroom. The literature shows that there is no one set way to train teachers. Instead, there is a scattershot selection of possible programs, only a few of which are geared toward preparing teachers for the high-need classrooms full of difficult students in urban environments that they are likely to face. Even within the programs that take the student population and environment into account, pre-service teachers are likely to be given information and experience that is not helpful and may even be detrimental to their teaching practice and are likely to end up isolated and often frustrated.

A new model of teacher training for pre-service and first year teachers, then, is needed. It must include a heavy focus on classroom management, since managing the classroom is perhaps the single most important aspect of teaching. (Oliver & Reschly, 2007) Gallup (2010) found that experienced teachers agree with this: they tend to have strong ideas of what kind of management helps their students succeed and be engaged in the classroom.

(Young, Crain, & McCullough, 1993) present a performance enhancement model that helps new teachers adjust once they get into the classroom, keeping them from feeling isolated and, even more importantly, helping them deal with the things that their pre-service training did not prepare them for, such as disciplinary issues. This type of teacher training model, perhaps with the addition of carefully selected student teaching placements, is the sort which can serve as a framework for the sort of program proposed in this dissertation.

Training Pre-Service Teachers on Developing Effective Communication and Public Relations Skills

Teachers clearly need to be trained in communication skills, both verbal and non-verbal. (Brackett et al, 2011) found that better relationship between teachers and their students can reduce poor behavior in the classroom. In many of the most difficult classrooms, students speak a wide variety of languages, and pre-service training does not always contain information on how to deal with this on a clearly linguistic level, as noted above (Cajker & Hall 2009). (Rubin & Feezel, 1986) found that the level of a teacher's communication skills is crucial, particularly for pre-service student teachers. In fact, the level of teachers' communication skills perceived by both the self and by others, can be a determinant in how successful the teacher is in a student teaching placement. Better communications skills, according to the perceptual theory of competence applied in this article, can lead to teachers both feeling more prepared for their own classrooms and being perceived as more competent by students, administrators, and parents. Successful student teachers (and, it follows, those that are more prepared for their own classroom assignments) are those with better communications skills.

Communication training given to teachers can provide a powerful tool in working with some of the most difficult students that a new teacher is likely to face in our integrated classrooms. (Carr & Durand, 1985) found that functional communication training, however, can help with bad behavior in the classroom. In this study, developmentally- disabled students who were trained to ask for teacher attention versus engaging in certain behaviors determined to the classroom environment (aggression and tantrums) were less likely to engage in these behaviors. This study points to the importance of functional communication. However, this study is limited due to the sample size of students (only four) that were studied, and also due to the fact that all were developmentally disabled. Due to a large number of students in today's mainstream classrooms who are emotionally or developmentally delayed or disturbed, this study points to an intriguing possible direction for further research. Durand's earlier work (Durand, 1990) also explores the idea of functional communication training for teachers and thence for students as a way to deter misbehavior. He found that this form of training, given to teachers, could successfully help them deal with students with a variety of behavioral and emotional diagnoses. Since this is exactly what the average inner-city novice teacher in particular faces in his or her classroom, this training is valuable not just for those who teach students who are in special placements, but for mainstream classroom teachers of every subject as well. (Kravitz, Kamps, Kemmerer, & Potucek, 2002) found that a picture system of communication, in which teachers could be trained, was especially useful for autistic students. Again, however, this study is limited by its small sample size. The number of students with a diagnosis on the autism spectrum in mainstream classrooms is certainly growing, and this too could prove an intriguing avenue for training for pre-service teachers if used more fully.

(Frymier & Houser, 2000) noted that the teacher-student relationship is just like any other interpersonal relationship. The authors surveyed students to find out what communications skills they considered to be most important in terms of evaluating the competency of their own teachers. A major one was referential communication, essentially the ability to interact in a meaningful way, not just giving orders but both giving and receiving information and reacting to information that is received as well. Both male and female students rated this dimension of communication as important, and both genders also felt that ego support was something important for teachers to engage in. Teachers who are trained in these communication and interpersonal skills are more successful than those who are not. (Murray, 2002) noted how important it is for students and teachers to have good relationships. Supportive relationships led to better self-concept and better overall social and emotional health for students with various high-incidence disabilities in this study. (Hughes & Cavell, 1999) found that good relationships with their teachers were also important for students who did not have a disability but merely presented with conduct problems, both in early childhood classrooms and in the later years of schooling. Significantly, a positive teacher-student relationship was found to be especially important for students whose mothers reported behaviors considered consistent with rejecting or neglecting their children. Since this is true of so many students in the highest-risk populations for school violence and bad behavior, this again underscores the huge importance of the student teacher relationship. The literature clearly shows how crucial this relationship is to good learning experiences for students, and teachers need to be taught accordingly to build this relationship.

Clearly, communication is important to what transpires in the classroom. However, the successful teacher must be able to communicate effectively with those outside of the classroom as well; doing a sort of "public relations" for his or herself and the work that is being done in the class. Numerous studies show that such outward-focused communication with parents and other stakeholders improves both academic and, perhaps even more significantly, the behavioral outcomes in the classroom. (Greenwood & Hickman, 1991) noted that teacher preparation for parent communication was, at the time of their study, insufficient and put together ten recommendations for teachers to learn to interact with parents in all of their capacities, including as volunteers and as teachers of their own children in the home and thus reinforces what is taught in the classroom. In the years since this study, teacher training in communications and public relations skills has increased with the goal of increasing parent, and thus student engagement in the classroom.

This is something that teacher training has increasingly evolved, over the intervening decades, to reflect. By explaining to parents and other stakeholders effectively what is going on in their classrooms through newsletters, phone calls, or other forms of frequent contact with the world outside the school, teachers can bring positive attention to their classroom, enhancing their careers and their students' learning experiences. Grants and other special opportunities are often available for teachers doing new and innovative things.

(Simich-Dudgeon, 1993) found that one of the indicators for student success is for teachers to know more about and to actively promote parent involvement, as well as involvement of other outside stakeholders. To do this effectively, teachers must be able to understand how to deal with the different sorts of parents they might encounter. Today's students in our urban public schools are perhaps more diverse than ever before, and the same is clearly true of their parents. The wide variety of family configurations, languages spoken, and cultural differences, and some families being dysfunctional, have a role to play in parent communication and in what parents may see as their role in that communication process. Understanding this via training in cultural differences (diversity training) is also a skill that teachers need, and luckily is one often addressed in pre-service and in-service teacher training. This particular sort of training will be discussed in more depth below.

Ultimately, the literature makes it clear that teachers are receiving some of the training they need in terms of communications skills. This is a positive thing. But it is equally clear that communications skills have a huge impact on every aspect of a teacher's classroom experience, from how the students behave to whether they disrupt the classroom and how they perceive their relationship with the teacher. These skills are also important from a public relations perspective, as teachers can improve their own and their students' outcomes by interacting effectively with the outside world. The importance of these factors mean that, while the training currently in place is adequate, more advanced training is needed, and communications and public relations skills must be a part of any revised training program for pre-service teachers.

Gary J. Rose, Ph.D.

Pre-service Teachers and Conflict Resolution Training

Another area of teacher training that must be addressed to create a complete and thorough overview of the literature is pre-service teacher training in conflict resolution. Conflict resolution skills have an obvious place in the classroom since one teacher is often asked to deal with thirty or more personalities all interacting together in a small space in each class, not to mention parents, colleagues, administrators, and other stakeholders. Effective teachers are those who have good conflict resolution skills and have been explicitly trained conflict productively (Marzano, 2001).

(Onchwari, 2010) found that many pre-service teachers did not feel confident in their pre-service training or in their ability to deal with stress in their students. Although this particular study concerned early childhood education, it can be extrapolated to apply to older students as well. Teachers who can recognize and diffuse stress are more successful in the classroom, so Onchwari's conclusion that more time should be spent teaching pre-service teachers skills in this area is certainly a valid observation.

(Carter, 2002) found that giving teachers conflict resolution skills can help them to connect with their students and can lead the students to adopt such modes of behavior as well, leading indirectly and directly to fewer conflicts in the classroom, whether these conflicts are among or between students or between students and teachers. Student satisfaction with their experience in school, as well as teacher satisfaction, is improved if teachers have better conflict resolution skills.

(Jenkins, Ritblatt, & McDonald, 2008) found that effective conflict resolution skills definitely have a place in the early childhood classroom in particular. In their study, teachers who had these skills and had been trained in them saw a marked difference in their classrooms. The educators perceived their classroom coping strategies and use of conflict resolution to be positive and to work well, leading to a better environment for the teacher and for the students. It is easy to extrapolate that these sorts of skills then might also lead to less teacher burnout.

Conflict resolution skills for teachers are not just useful in the classroom, however. Teachers trained in conflict resolution can work better with colleagues and other school stakeholders as well. In a case study of English-speaking educators teaching English at a Japanese school, teachers who had better conflict resolution skills fit in better and had more positive experiences with their jobs (Torpey, 2006). While not all cultural differences among colleagues are as large or striking as the ones in this case study, it is clear that conflict resolution training plays a key part in preparing teachers for productive careers in the schools where they are assigned in terms of their interactions outside the classroom as well as those within the classroom.

(Sparks & Hammond, 1981) found that teachers who were better in tune with their own stressors, such as conflicts in the classroom, and better able to deal with them, had longer and more successful teaching careers and reported higher job and life satisfaction as well. (Jennings & Greenberg, 2009) refer to this as a part of a teacher's social and emotional competence, and teachers with higher levels in this measure, according to their study, do better in the classroom and teach more effectively. Conflict is inevitable in the classroom and in the school building as a whole, but with good conflict resolution skills, teachers are able to deal with it and to continue their teaching practice, making for a better school environment for themselves and their students alike. (Girard, 1995) holds a similarly positive view of teachers being taught conflict resolution skills. She states that they can improve the school climate overall as well as the individual teachers' classroom environments and student outcomes, but cautions that these findings have limited utility if these skills are not taught throughout a teacher's career, beginning in pre-service. While much of the available literature addresses conflict resolution training without pointing out when it is best used, Girard fills this gap, recommending that it be a crucial part of pre-service training for all teachers. In the years since Girard's study, this has indeed become more and more of the norm in teacher training. Girard's idea that conflict resolution training should not be intended just for individual teachers, but school and even district-wide certainly has a place in the design of any new training program for teachers or indeed for any adults hoping to work in today's classrooms.

Most significantly, (Gagnon & Leone, 2001) make explicit the connection between teacher's conflict resolution skills and training and the prevention of violence in schools. While their study comes from before the spate of school shootings in the first years of the millennium, their point that conflict resolution skills are a good preventer of school violence still applies. At the time the authors wrote, they proved that school violence was on the decline by citing many statistics, including some from the Federal Bureau of Investigation. The public perception, according to the authors, that school violence was increasing was not supported by reality. Nowadays, however, the opposite is true, and school violence is increasing to previously unseen levels, as indicated by the Lanza case referenced in the introduction. (Rozalski, Drasgow, & Yell, 2009) found that even among violent young offenders, good conflict management and resolution strategies, along with strong relationships between students and adults, made for better experiences for all concerned. Now, more than ever Gagnon & Leone's inclusion of conflict resolution as an important aspect of teacher training rings true.

(Skovholt, Cognetta, Ye, & King, 1997) also stress conflict management and resolution training as a tool for preventing school violence of all kinds, including bullying as well as the more obviously violent incidents, like school shootings, which have become such a problem in recent years. Unfortunately, according to this study, the programs that are put into place to train both teachers and students regarding conflict resolution in inner city schools are too often created by those who are out of touch with the reality of urban schools: being mainly white, middle-class administrators and educators with little experience of the urban schools in which they wish the training to work. This is something that must be addressed in a new training program for teachers.

A third area that pre-service teachers receive training in is cultural diversity and tolerance. This is important in urban schools in particular for many reasons. The urban, inner-city schools, where violence is common, are those which are most likely to contain a culturally diverse population. (Quiroz, Greenfield, & Altchech, 2003) point out the parent-teacher conference as one way to bridge this gap, but teachers need to receive explicit pre-service training on how to do this. (McAllister & Irvine, 2000) note three process-oriented ways to make this and other culturally responsive teaching best practices, providing a model for how to train teachers to work effectively and sensitively with different cultures.

(Bennett, 2013) posits that pre-service field placements for student teaching can positively impact the cultural understanding and readiness of new teachers for teaching in culturally diverse situations. She found that tutoring diverse students in an after-school program, as a field placement that was part of pre-service education, was useful for eight pre-service teachers, who reported higher understanding of other cultures than before they began the placement. Culturally responsive pedagogy became something they understood on an active level, not just something they had read about and understood abstractly from the classroom instruction they had received. Bennet concluded that these teachers were better prepared than they previously had been to take on the challenge of teaching in an urban, diverse environment. (McDonald et al., 2011) had similar findings in their study of community-based organizations as potential field placements for pre-service teachers. Would-be teachers who were placed there had a better understanding of the cultural community and of the diversity of the students they later taught.

(Larke, 1990) created useful tool for assessing pre-service teachers' cultural competency: a scale that assessed elementary school teachers of various ethnicities both before and after completing a cultural education course. The survey found that the course was useful, but the scale itself is also an important piece of the literature as the academic establishment considers how to measure and how to teach cultural tolerance and diversity to pre-service teachers as well as to those already on the job. Clearly, assessing and teaching cultural competence is an important part of pre-service teacher training, and the extant literature reflects that this is already a priority within teacher education.

Gary J. Rose, Ph.D.

Summary

Training for pre-service teachers has a wide variety of foci, including the subject matter that each individual teacher will eventually teach. Beyond content knowledge, though, there is only moderate consensus in the extant literature about what future teachers really need to know. Some scholars advocate student teaching placements, both to promote cultural sensitivity and for other reasons, while others believe that these are not useful. What is clear is that a balance between theoretical and practical education will best address the problem of teacher burnout and help teachers to be successful in their new classrooms.

Pre-service teachers need three kinds of education, which they are receiving in different training programs to various extents. (NCATE, 2010 & CAEP 2011) One of these is cultural diversity training, which a wide variety of literature cites as important for educator success. Conflict resolution skills are also something that should be taught, since they have been shown to be a viable strategy for reducing undesirable behavior and even violence in schools. Finally, communication skills need to be imparted to teachers, so that they can perform outreach on their own and their students' behalf, interact better with students and with parents, and solve problems that might arise in the classroom or in the workplace as a whole. These facets of teacher pre-service education are important, and sufficient literature exists to prove their worth. It follows, then, that these must be a part of any proposed new program for pre-service teacher training. However, examining the literature, it is clear that there are also missing pieces, from which teachers could benefit.

"You can learn great things from your mistakes when you aren't busy denying them."

CHARACTERISTICS OF AT-RISK STUDENTS

But this is all fine and good you say, but I am already a certified teacher. You may agree that you did not get the proper training you need to deal with "at-risk" students as stated in chapter 3, and yes, you realize that there is a difference between traditional students and "at-risk" students. But, specifically, what are the differences and how can you overcome them, when you have an entire classroom of struggling individuals?

Students at risk, include those that have a high percentage drop out rate. They typically have a history of academic failure which adds to their situation at home re. dysfunctional families. Statistics show that many of their poor academic performance goes all the way back to the third grade. (K. L. Alexander, Entwisle, & Dauber, 1995; Garnier, Stein, & Jacobs, 1997). They have poor reading and study skills, which parlay into poor achievement scores. (BattinPearson et al., 2000; Jozefowicz, Arbreton, Eccles, Barber, & Colarossi, 1994; Raber, 1990; L. Steinberg et al., 1984; Wilkinson & Frazer, 1990). As previously stated,

Characteristics of At-Risk Students

emotional and behavioral problems compound their problems, leading to self-esteem issues. Because some of them sense the difference in their non-at-risk fellow students, they are prone to cause discipline problems in class, use drugs, and engage in criminal activities (Finn, 1991; Garnier et al., 1997; Jozefowicz et al., 1994; Rumberger, 1995; U.S. Dept. of Education, 1992). This anti-social behavior causes many of them to hang out with other peers labeled as at-risk or juvenile delinquents. (Battin-Pearson et al., 2000; Hymel, Comfort, SchonertReichl, & McDougall, 1996). Feeding off each other, these fellow at-risk peers reinforce their dislike for school and for any academic settings. The school setting no longer has a place for them in their life. Sadly, it is around this time frame that gang affiliation becomes a possibility. (Christenson & Thurlow, 2004; Hymel et al., 1996; Rumberger, 1995).

This peer association with other at-risk youth, can lead to cutting school, deliberate disruption in the classroom so they can be suspended or expelled, drug and alcohol use, and criminal activity.

By this time, most educators have given up on their "at-risk - I don't give a damn" students. They are eventually suspended or expelled or, due to their criminal activity, find themselves either placed on probation or doing time in juvenile detention facilities. Now they become your responsibilities. If you noticed, I did not say, your headaches.

Gary J. Rose, Ph.D.

Generally speaking, students are engaged in their classwork and education when they:
- participate in all areas of the school including academic, social and extracurricular activities (behavioral engagement)
- feel included in the school and have feelings of belonging to the school (emotional engagement)
- are personally invested in and take ownership of their learning (cognitive engagement).

"At-risk" students are disengaged, meaning that they do not demonstrate any of these characteristics, and/or they are not enrolled or have very poor school attendance. Presence of only some of these characteristics may indicate a child or young person is at risk of disengagement.

There is a range of factors that may contribute to a child or young person becoming disengaged or at risk of disengaging from school. These include:
- **Family and community factors** such as poverty, parental unemployment and/or low educational attainment, homelessness, transience or living in out-of-home care, refugee background, family breakdown/relationship issues, and domestic violence.
- **Personal factors** such as physical or mental health issues, disability, behavioral issues, offending behavior and/or contact with police or justice system, substance misuse or dependency,

pregnancy or parenting, caring responsibilities, and learning difficulties.
- **School-related factors** such as negative relationships with teachers or peers, unsupportive school culture, limited subject options and lack of student participation in decision making.

Young people may often experience multiple risk factors, which may be interdependent. For example, family breakdown may be a factor in substance misuse, which may itself contribute to other problems such as offending behavior.

The impact of risk factors on engagement, health, and wellbeing will vary between individuals, depending on their levels of resilience and protective factors such as support from a trusted adult. While the presence or one or more risk factor does not inevitably mean a child or young person will become disengaged, it is important that schools have an awareness of these factors to be able to identify and address issues as early as possible.

So, what indicators should you and your school look out for as signs of possible disengagement leading to the label of "at-risk"? Indicators would include:
- erratic or no attendance
- low literacy or numeracy/poor attainment
- lack of interest in school and/or stated intention to leave
- negative interactions with peers

- behavioral issues including aggression, violence, or social withdrawal
- significant change in behavior, attitude or performance.

Schools can draw on a range of data and tools to identify students that are at risk of disengagement. These may include:
- information on family background, educational history and personal issues collected at the time of enrolment
- attendance data
- educational, health or welfare assessments completed by in-school or Department support services (and external support services where these have been provided to the school with the student and their parents' consent)
- reports from classroom teachers on learning and behavioral issues

For over 20 years, I have been asked, why do I teach at-risk students, both juvenile and adults? It's easy to answer. I love the challenge and the reward of showing them that they are not losers and can turn their lives around. Does it always work? No, but I can't count the number of successes I have had over the years, versus failures.

At the beginning of his book, I told you that when you run into your at-risk students years later and they come up to you and thank you for helping them turns

Characteristics of At-Risk Students

their lives around from a life a crime or death, you will love the accolades you receive.

Now, understanding what common characteristics at-risk students have, how will you attempt to teach them? To me, the best way to answer this is to review what the experts feel, makes a great teacher. Why? Because in my opinion, you must be a great teacher or at least be on the top of your game, to succeed in teaching at-risk students. It has always amazed me through my many years of teaching, how the "Teacher of the Year" award, rarely goes to Alternative Education teachers. You have the toughest students in your district, all placed in your classroom, and if you do your job, you will help turn them around and graduate high school. Yet you will rarely be viewed as a candidate for Teacher of the Year. That award will go to a teacher assigned to a traditional school

"Improvise, Adapt and Overcome"

WHAT MAKES A GREAT TEACHER?

On their website Great Schools (www.greatschools.org/gk/articles/what-makes-a-great-teacher), the following are listed as characteristics of a great teacher. I will use those characteristics and see how they apply to the teaching of at-risk students.

What makes a great teacher? Not taking anything away from other careers, teaching is a very complicated job today. You not only have to have knowledge of your subject matter and curriculum, but you also must have a handle of your states standards. You must enter your classroom with enthusiasm and a caring attitude. But that is not enough. You must have knowledge of your discipline and classroom management techniques. Frankly, you must love what you are trying to achieve, the academic advancement of your students.

I have been around a lot of teachers who have excellent knowledge of their particular discipline, but sadly, they do not have the ability to present this material in a manner that encourages their students to learn and apply it to modern day situations. In other words, they have the ability but not the talent, to present or teach the material in a manner that their students can relate too. Placing these highly educated and knowledgeable teachers in front of at-risk students is a disaster in the making as I will allude to shortly.

"Great Teachers Set High Expectations for all Students"

If you go into your classroom of at-risk students, whether they are incarcerated or not, with the attitude that these are the "rejects" of the student population in your district, you are doing yourself and them a disservice. You will quickly realize that they are sizing you up to see what you are made of and what they can possibly get away with. These students will require a lot of energy that you probably would not have to expand in a traditional classroom. If you cannot tolerate rude, disrespectful, mouthy, and in some cases, students with a hatred for authority, you will find yourself regretting you entered this field of education.

I realize that as a former law enforcement officer, I gained a lot of excellent training in dealing with out of control situations, unruly individuals, drug and alcohol intoxicated people, violent, disturbed and mentally ill individuals, as well as people in extremely psychological crisis including hostage negotiations. That does not mean that you too, cannot learn how to combat these similar situations you come across in your classroom.

I also realized over the years that our students want to learn, providing you do so in a manner that is entertaining. Think about it. They want instant communication via their cell phones and social media. They play video games and, win or lose, quickly want to move on to the next game. When they watch movies, even in my classroom, unless I set them up, they want to see actions, adventure, and special effects etc. Don't believe me? Without telling them the movie you are going to show them, make it a black and white film and see what their reactions will be. They will be turned off from the start and you will start losing control of your classroom.

Does that mean you can never show a black and white film? No, but you must get them to "buy-into" why you want them to watch it and what they can expect to get out of it.

I make a statement at the beginning of each school year or semester or quarter, about the expectations I have of them, but you may be surprised, that I do not do this first. Instead, I do the following:

Good morning everyone. Some of you I have had before, welcome back, I guess (wait for some laughter). Welcome to Alder Grove Court and Community School. I have found in all the years I have attended school, that I really appreciated my teachers, professors etc., who shared with me, their background, expectations and whatever else they felt like sharing, so that I could get a better read about what "makes them tick," what biases they may have so I knew where they were coming from on various topics.

What Makes a Great Teacher?

As I say this, I am constantly establishing eye contact with each student. Those that glance away are the ones you will need to concentrate on. Are they just being rude and feel that you are just full of it, or are they introverts and shy.

I continue, "*My name is Dr. Gary Rose, and I will be your instructors for the next ( ) months. I was born and raised in the bay area and moved up to the Auburn area after my dad, whom my family and I lost ( ) years ago, due to a bad heart.* Again, pause for effect. You must project yourself as an actor and you are performing for them. You want to get a hook into them. Some of them are probing for any weakness they can spot. Again, they are sizing you up. Do not make your pauses too long, or you will start to lose some of them.

"*I am a retired police sergeant having worked for the Milpitas Police Department near San Jose if you don't know where it is, and after getting injured, had to retire. It was during my profession as a police officer, that I first got a chance to experience the role of a teacher. You see, I worked two tours of duty working undercover narcotics. My hair was as long as (pointing to a student) and I had a full beard and mustache. If I remember, someday I will bring in a picture of what I looked like.*" Normally I would get a lot of "Yeah, that would be cool."

"*The chief of police did not want to put me directly back on the street after working undercover for 2 ½ years, so instead he placed me in our Community Relations Division, to decompress from riding motorcycles and dealing with drug dealers. One of the responsibilities* *as a Community Relations officer, was to teach in our schools, starting in kindergarten and, skipping a grade – you know, 2nd grade, 4th grade and so on, a grade related topic. For kindergartens' it was Dangerous Strangers – Red light, Green light. Do you know what that means?* I ask this to judge how many are paying attention.

Finally, at the high school level, I taught a 5-unit course in Police Science. That is where I started experiencing the excitement and responsibilities of being a teacher. Pause, followed by, *"I got injured on a man with a gun call, and had to retire. Due to most of my police experience being an investigator, I teamed up with a fellow retired police sergeant and together we formed a polygraph – police background investigation firm. I earned my first master's degree in Human Behavior. Did that for almost 5 years but got bored, began studying and passed my stockbroker examination. Made my money in the stock market as a financial advisor but once again, got bored. I was still going to school and eventually earned my second master's degree in Social Psychology. Boredom set in again, I guess because I have a type A personality, so I decided that I wanted to explore being a substitute teacher at the high school level.*

After finding out what hoops I had to jump through, I passed my licensing exams and became a teacher. My supervisor felt that my law enforcement background made me a fit in juvenile hall, so I was assigned there for over 12 years until I was instructed to set up the Alder Grove Academy – a military style boot camp school where my students wore U.S. Army Battle Dress uniforms".

What Makes a Great Teacher?

Wait for the comments –"*God, I wish we could wear uniforms. That would be so cool. Hell, I don't want to wear uniforms*" etc.

"*I finished my doctorate in Social Psychology and taught both at the college and university level and still work with the University of Delaware with graduate students.*

"*Well, that's about it. Thank you for not snoring.*" What for the laughter to subside.

Now this is my style. What I told them is the information I chose to share. It is up to you regarding your opening introduction and how much information you want your students to know about you.

I then apologize in advance if I mispronounced their names while taking attendance. Once completed, I point to my agenda posted on the board. For some, this may seem overwhelming, especially if they have been out of school for some time. As I go through the agenda, I try to give them a few examples of the fun things we will do to get through the subject matter. I normally skipped P/E since I will explain later, how that is not a given and must be earned.

This is the transition time I use to issue their lab notebooks, have them divide up columns for the various subjects I just reviewed from the board, and then have them fill in their (A) grades.

You may want to then ask them to write a short essay about themselves, telling them they can share whatever they wish and that probably you shared too much; again, thanking them for not following asleep.

I may interject a warning for those the just sit there and do not start writing that, *"Those who do not want to write, will be asked to make a verbal essay to the class."* That normally gets everyone working.

Great Teachers Have Clear, Written-out Objectives

My agenda spells out for my at-risk students, exactly what we will be covering each day. Some teachers like to handout documents that outlines their agenda, class rules, grading and so on.

Initially, I did not do this, but as time went on, part of my style of getting my students to buy-in to my style of teaching, was to inform them that I would be running my classroom similar to what they can expect in college. Since I taught there, they knew I had experience.

Dealing primarily with high school aged students and later incarcerated adults, I found that giving them a syllabus was a first for many of them and they appreciated knowing what to expect in college. My syllabus included my name; email address through the county website which is also distributed to parents/guardians, courses, grading, normal bell schedule, and future projects or research papers. Included was the schedule of their weekly exam.

No school rules? In juvenile hall, the rules are pretty much established by the probation department.

What Makes a Great Teacher?

Teachers assigned to this institution were told the rules and we followed them. Before an assault on a teacher, we issued regular sized pencils and would conduct a count at the beginning of each section. We would recount when the students turned them in for breaks, and finally recount them at the end of the day.

Remember how at-risk students will probe for weaknesses? One morning, my teaching assistant and I walked into our unit and was informed by the probation officers assigned to our unit, that they found a pencil in one of the cells. We could not figure out how this happened since we counted the pencils at the end of the day and all were account for. Well, as it turned out, one of the at-risk students, broke his pencil in half. After asking for permission to sharpen his pencil, sharpened both ends. He turned in one part of the pencil at the end of the day, which we took as having all pencils accountable for; but instead, an "extra" pencil made it to his cell. Sneaky.

Large pencils were eventually replaced with smaller golf pencils after a probation officer was stabbed and a teacher injured trying to rescue the officer.

Another example of students probing for weaknesses in the system you set up in your classroom, was the time probation found orange peelings stuff behind the computer towers on the floor beneath the shelving on which the computers were located. The plan, which the incarcerated juveniles did in the past, was to take the orange peels as well as some graphite from their pencils that they shaved off and rolled up in their underwear, back to their cells. There, they would use whatever they could to poke holes into their skin, rub in the graphite and then apply the oil (acidic) from the orange peel, creating a "prison" tattoo.

Taking these and other examples I could cite, I realized that writing out rules and placing them on the walls of the classroom, was a waste of time. At the high school level, your kids already know common courtesy, even from their dysfunctional family life, so why waste the time and energy placing rules on the wall. Besides, there are some at-risk students that will take these postings of rules as a challenge, to see, up to that point, you will tolerate a slight violation of a rule before it is deemed a violation. I feel the same about posting expected behavior, which proponents of some of the latest behavior modification theorists, are forcing teachers to utilize.

I would say to my students, "*Ok, now, I want to review the rules of the classroom.*" Get ready for the groans, complaints and disgusted looks. Some students may even start shouting out rules like no gum, no running in the classroom, no swearing, no hitting, and so on. Let them throw out these rules. It just verifies that now in their academic life, they know all of the rules. After they get it all out of their system, that is when I would state, "*There is only one rule in my classroom.*" Establish eye contact, because you have thrown them a curveball that many did not expect. "*The only rule in my classroom is that everyone shows respect for everyone else. And, since I am part of the *classroom, that goes for me. If someone does something wrong that does not show me respect, we will have a problem. Any questions?"*

You will be surprised. They were not ready for this "one rule" classroom presentation. Think about it. Lets' say you are teaching in traditional school. I can assure you that they have probably heard or even created classroom rules for every class and now they must do it again with you.

Instead, you have already told them that you will be treating them as future college students and with that, comes respect for themselves and others. Some of my colleagues liked my idea and have seen it worked, that they have taken down their classroom rules and replaced it with a simple "Respect" on their classroom walls.

Great Teachers are Prepared and Organized

Although I feel that what I have stated so far is important, this is probably number one. I have witnessed so many teachers crash and burn in their first year of teaching, that they either leave the field of teaching or absolutely hate teaching, which, by the way, will be perceived by your students. I have also seen special education teachers, reassigned into the at-risk population due to budget cuts, torn to shreds by students, even though these teachers were bright, well educated, and knew their material. So, how did the at-risk students get to them? They were not prepared and organized.

At-risk students will probe and continue to probe to find any weaknesses you have. When a teacher is not prepared or organized, "at-risks" students will interpret this as a sign of weakness and will quickly jump at the opportunity you gave them to act out in class causing a classroom disturbance that can easily get out of hand. Simply turning your back routinely can give your students the timing they need to throw an object, hit a classmate, throw a spitball, you name it.

The unprepared and unorganized teacher now must spend their precious instructional time to devise a way to get the classroom back in order. If your students sense that you are getting frustrated or, better yet, they are getting under your skin, they will relish in continuing their behavior. In one case, I heard that the students, sensing that they had their teacher "on-the-ropes," began questioning her as to her ability to be a teacher. They began mocking her lecture delivery. They mimicked her talking, the way she stood in the classroom. They accused her of having favorites, that she didn't care about them. Even telling her that she was the worst teacher they ever had and that she should quit. The teacher said it was like a snowball going downhill with each student adding on to the size of the ball. She had to leave the classroom and retreated to the teacher's bathroom where it took some time for her to stop crying and regain composure. But, she had to return to the classroom. Is there a solution to avoiding this from happening to you?

Yes, it is called being prepared and organized. It means that you must have more than your students could complete in the time allotted, thus they must stay focused and not have time to exploit any weaknesses you may have.

The night before my next day of teaching, I would always have a general idea as to what I would be teaching during each block (agenda). For example, in Algebra, I would first explain what we are going to learn during the block of time. I would place an equation on the board and instead of asking for a volunteer to solve it, I would instead explain the steps involved. My students were expected to take notes showing the steps in the solution process and then I would issue each of them, problems to solve. I had already placed weaker Algebra students with more accomplished students and allowed them to work together, while I walked the room, making sure everyone was working.

You will always have some smarter students finish their assignment and think that now they can do whatever they want since they are done. Not so fast. I already anticipated this and had extra, more difficult problems for them to solve. No use rushing because Mr. Rose always seemed to have more material. Using this approach for all your subject matter will stop you from having downtime which, as illustrated above, will give your students time to act out.

Gary J. Rose, Ph.D.

Great Teachers have Command Presence

I want to cover what we call in law enforcement, your command presence in the classroom. Do not teach from your desk. That makes you too predictable for your students. They know where you are and can anticipate when you are looking down or otherwise distracted from them. Instead, walk around the room. Look at everyone's work, but while doing so, quickly glance around, especially at your known troublemakers. This keeps them off balance and makes you, unpredictable. It will not take long before your at-risk students realize that you are wise to their games, so why play it. Might as well do what the teacher wants or no P/E or fun Fridays after their exam.

My students, when they walked into the classroom, always saw a huge amount of material on either my desk or on a chair. They realized after only a few days, that there will ALWAYS be work to do. They never knew that in the middle was a lot of scratch paper that I used for effect.

Again, admitting that I am old school, I believe that your dress in the classroom is also extremely important. You will be in front of your students for six to seven hours and at-risk students will observe everything you do and wear. Part of your job as a teacher is to act as a role model and this starts with what you wear. It comes under the curriculum of teaching life skills.

At the Alder Grove Academy where my cadets wore U.S. Army camouflage, they insisted that I also wear a uniform. They knew that I would never ask them to do anything that I would not do, so I wore a black battle dressed uniform all the way down to black polished combat boots.

In juvenile hall, I initially wore what I would have chosen to wear if attending a church service. But having to carry a set of heavy keys and chain to open doors, made wearing a suit impractical so my dress was normally a pair of slacks or Dockers and a pullover shirt.

While teaching in front of college and university students including my incarcerated adults, I felt that I needed to project a more scholarly image and always wore a suit. Amazingly each class usually started off with both male and female students complimenting me on my choice of shirt and/or tie color. Believe me, it makes your job a whole lot easier since it shows your students that you care about them, all the way down to how you dress. It also helps in keeping their attention, such as them constantly noticing my Rolex watch. Be aware that many at-risk incarcerated students, both juvenile and adult, male and female, are very manipulative. They will try all kinds of psychological ploys on you.

Let me share a story with you to illustrate my point about your dress code. Years ago, the Alternative Education departments from Northern California attended a conference in hopes of collaboratively coming up with strategies to aid our high school students in passing the California High School Exit

Exam. Pass rates were abysmal and it was hoped that this get-together, would help us breakdown the components of the exam and better teach to the test.

It was going to be a two-day event in a large hotel so I decided to wear a new pair of black Levis and pullover golf shirts. My colleagues, both male and female also dress casually.

There was a stir in the large auditorium with the arrival of teachers from a not-to-be named county office. Attention was diverted to them since many wore old clothes, displayed large amounts of tattoos, and some of the male teachers wore pants so low they displayed what I call "butt cleavage," when discussing proper dress to my students before they go to a job interview.

That image has always stuck to me and one day I asked my incarcerated adult students if I was wrong in my judgment that day? Many of them commented that perhaps these teachers were making up for their weaknesses as educators in front of their students, by trying to be one of them. I had just shown them a DVD entitled, *The Corruption of the American Child,"* in which the commentator posited that many parents, instead of acting as role models for their children, instead want to be their friends and skirt their responsibilities of making proper choices such as dress. Perhaps they were correct in their assessments.

Therefore, it is important to us as educators, who for the most part, spend more waking hours with our students than their own parents, to act as their role models and dress appropriately.

To project a role model image, make it part of your daily routine to dress in a professional manner. Personal hygiene is a must. Remember, at-risk students upon initially meeting you will try to find anything they can use to get under your skin.

In summary, show your students what you will be covering in the different blocks for the day. Do not become predictable in your delivery, where you stand, where you look. Keep them off balanced. Always have too much material to complete. You can always use it the next time. Always stress to your students the importance of their grades and the Friday exam. If they screw around today, they will have a hard time passing the weekly test.

Great Teachers Engage Students and Get Them to Look at Issues in A Variety of Ways

I told my students that the reason I will be running my classroom like a college or university classroom, is that I want them to feel comfortable day one, when they enter a lecture hall or a large classroom with maybe a hundred or more students would be attending. One of the big reasons (and I have many that I will share later) that I despise Common Core, is the movement away from the Socratic method of teaching which is prevalent in most of our institutions of higher learning.

Gary J. Rose, Ph.D.

To engage at-risk students, besides "entertaining" them, you must show them the relevance the topic has for them in the "real world." Lets' use the topic of the Salem witchcraft trials as an example; a U.S. history topic that I liked to teach around Halloween. It always seemed appropriate to me to teach it around this time of the year, and there are so many other topics and exercises that can be spun from it.

First, I would ask the class, whom among them, believes in ghosts, witches, warlocks, superstitions and so on. Be prepared for your class to seem a little out of control for a little while. Let them share, let them shout out of their responses. When you are ready, just stand up in front of the class with your arms crossed, they will get the message. Someone may even apologize for the class. Thank them for their enthusiasm and then continue.

This is how easy it was during this time in American and European history to be labeled a witch. Remember, if a person walked out into a field and saw a rat run from behind a rock, it was believed that this rock, created rats. Everything that went right or wrong was attributed to God. You damn a person verbally, and later a wheel falls off his wagon, and you could be label a person dealing in the black arts – witchcraft. You should get a few laughs. After they subside, go on. *"You don't believe how easy it would be to be labeled a witch? Let me show you. Those that have long sleeves on, please roll them up to at least your elbow."* Start walking around the room.

What Makes a Great Teacher?

I always liked to pick on the most popular students in the class first.

Looking at a student's arm and noticing a mark (doesn't really matter what is it), I would shriek out loud, while pointing to the mark, *"The mark of the devil! The mark of the devil!* Your students will start busting up and most will start self-examining their arms before you get to them. After naming several "witches" in the classroom, I would then look at them and asked them, similarly to the witchcraft court, *Be thee a witch?"* I would tell them to say no. Yes, you will have some that say, "Yes, I am a witch," in an attempt to throw you off balance.

Again, using a popular student, I would then use trial by ordeal to see if they were or were not a witch. I would draw a teeter-totter drawing on the board and list the names of two other students to "sit" on one side of the apparatus. The accused "witch" was tied to the opposite side. The "witch" was hanging over a lake, stream or another body of water. I would again ask her, "Be thee a witch?" and on cue, he/she would say no. Feel free to make fun of your own drawings. Don't worry, your students will comment as you draw the teeter-totter and your stick figures.

At that point, I would illustrate the two other students getting off their side of the
teeter -totter, allowing the accused to go under water. And then, I would glance at my watch as if I cared about the passing time. After a few minutes,

Gary J. Rose, Ph.D.

someone in the classroom would say, "Hey, Mr. Rose, she is probably drowned by now."

I would respond with, *Oh, I forgot to tell you. If she floated, she was a witch. She did not float, so she was innocent of witchcraft. She's dead, but she is not a witch.*" Get ready for the "what?" "That's tight?" "That's so wrong."

Sometimes I would then show them the movie *The Crucible* to get their comments about, in the play's rendition of the actual events, how easy it was for the afflicted girls to name someone a witch. Now, how will I get my students to look at these events in a different light?

I would then introduce the Hitler Youth movement and how these indoctrinated children were encouraged to name anyone, who was not a supporter of Hitler and to report them to the Gestapo for a reward. Do they think something like this could happen again? Or ask the question if it is happening now in the United States or other parts of the world? I have now made the study of U.S. history of the past (Salem Witchcraft Trials), compared them to the Hitler Youth movement, and now asked them to explore the current world and determine if history is repeating itself during their lifetime.

As promised, at the back of the book I will give you a lot of exercises similar to this that you can use to engage your students, forcing them to think abstractly (a requirement in higher education), and most importantly, have fun with them.

What Makes a Great Teacher?

Great Teachers Form Strong Relationships with Their Students and Show That They Care About Them as People

Great teachers have a knack for showing respect for their students, in return for their respect. You need to be judged as warm, enthusiastic, and accessible. That means that sometimes, you might have to stay later after school and make yourself available to students and parents who need them. In the Academy, my students knew that I got to school while they were still sleeping and that they could come in and meet with me before, during, and after school. This even turned into our own version of *Breakfast Club*, where several students, either struggling with Algebra or other subjects, meet at 6 AM to have breakfast with me while working on their subjects. In continuation high schools, there generally is not a lot of involvement in school-wide committees and after-school activities since you probably will not have a sports program or pep rallies etc. Working with at-risk students will physically and mentally drain you, so I am glad we did not have a lot of those extracurricular things to worry about. Except for school-site council committee and IEP meetings, there were very few activities after school.

Another way to form a close relationship with you at-risk students is to be *real*. By this, I mean, show signs of being human and not the all mighty authoritarian figure. This may sound strange coming from a retired police sergeant in a classroom, surrounded by at-risk students, but I did practice it and still do with my adult incarcerated students in the county jail.

Here is an example. *"Good morning guys and gals. I had a tough night last night with my old cat, Banshee, that is dying. I stayed awake with her until finally, she passed away."* Wait for the sadness, tears etc., to subside and then ...." *Thank you for your condolences, but I have a favor to ask. Since I have not had a lot of sleep, can you promise me that we will have a good day, have fun, and learn something so that I can go home on time and get some rest?"*

Something this innocent, coming from your heart, will build a strong relationship with your students. It's like your opening introduction in which you share whatever you feel comfortable sharing with them. Don't forget to add some jokes in if you can. People who laugh with you, have a hard time hating you.

Beware!

I had a Mexican male cadet come to me one day just before Christmas break. He had anger management issues and had assaulted a teacher and other classmates resulting in him be assigned to my boot camp school. He strived in the military type environment of the academy and relished the physical training and leadership courses presented by the army staff.

"Mr. Rose, do you need someone to help take care of your yard at home? I told him no since I had a weekly landscaping service take care of those chores.

What Makes a Great Teacher?

"Mr. Rose, I really need to make some money so that I can buy my mom a leather jacket for Christmas. Do you know where I can make some money?"

I told him that leather jackets cost a lot of money and with Christmas only ten days away, he did not have much time. He told me that the jacket he wanted to buy her wasn't real leather and that he could purchase it at Target if he could get it before they sell out.

Then, with tears in his eyes, he tells me that his mother was recently diagnosed with a brain tremor and was dying. I told him I was so sorry and made a deal with him. If he continued to do well at the academy and stayed out of trouble so to avoid violation of his probation, I would buy him the jacket for his mom. Before I could react, he quickly grabbed me in a bear hug. We set up a time after class the next day to purchase the coat.

We purchased the faux leather jacket and I drove him home. He saw that his mom was home so he asked me to drop him off down the street from his house so that he could sneak into his bedroom window. He and his sister, he told me, would wrap the jacket up and place it under their Christmas tree.

During Christmas break, my teaching assistant called me and said that he was incarcerated back in the juvenile detention facility and was going to be deported. I was crushed, but a realist that some people can't or refuse to change.

Returning from two weeks off, several of the cadets, males and females, came up to my desk and asked if I had heard about this student, that he was back in juvenile hall. I told them that I did not know the circumstances of his arrest, nor could I discuss it with them if I knew. I did state that he hurt me, knowing that one of my favorite students who seemed to be turning his life around, was now back in custody.

Then one of them asked me if I bought a leather jacket for this student's mom? I said I had and asked why? I thought that perhaps there were going to give me a bad time of becoming a softy. Instead what they told me hurt and angered me at the same time.

It was all a scam. His mother did not have a brain tumor nor was she sick. Instead, as I was told, she asked her son to ask me to buy a jacket for her and together they came up with the sob story of her impending death due to a brain tumor.

I never saw this student again nor did I go to the juvenile detention facility to confront him: instead, a lesson learned. Be prepared to get hurt after you develop a relationship with some of your students as illustrated above.

Great Teachers Are Masters of Their Subject Matter

Earlier I shared that I have worked with some brilliant teachers who were well versed in the subject matter of their discipline. Unfortunately, in some cases, they hated teaching students who were either struggling or did not show them the respect they felt they deserved. Part of the problem I felt, was that they were never taught either in their teaching colleges or during student teaching, that knowledge of subject matter, does not make them a great teacher.

I agree with the late Jaime Escalante, who told me that he never found one textbook that did it all. Instead, he believed that a great teacher must spend time continuing to gain new knowledge in their field: and take advantage of new findings, new discoveries. Keep abreast of current events. Read inspirational stories of other great teachers and how they attained the title "Great Teacher."

A great teacher must also present their material in an enthusiastic manner and instill a passion in their students to learn more on their own. I will give you an example shortly.

Additionally, you must possess the ability to entertain your students while instructing them. How do you do this? You need to have what I call a "hook." A strategy in which you get your students desiring more information. Call it what you want. A carrot and a stick. Bait and switch. A con job. Whatever.

While teaching at-risk students, I found that many of them are poor readers and writers, and getting them to complete a five-paragraph essay is a tough task. Fortunately, I was comfortable financially while teaching at the Academy, and needed to come up with a research paper idea that would get most of them excited about completing. I created a writing assignment, in which, no more than a team of two cadets, would listen to the words of a famous past "oldie but goodie," and research the lyrics in relation to the history taking place at the time the song was produced.

The song I chose was *Eve of Destruction*. When the students came back from their lunch break, I had an old boom-box on my desk that contained a copy of the song. I explained the rules of the contest. To get them hooked, I told them that the top prize winner(s) would receive $100. Second prize winners would receive $75. Third prize was $50. All the winners would also be invited to have dinner with me at our local Applebee's.

Wait for the banter to calm down by just staring at them, and once the classroom is yours' again, explain what they would be judged in the contest.

I then played the song. Some of my top students could pick out some of the lyrical meanings, but most could not. Their job was to use whatever means at their disposal, to research the meanings of the lyrics and then compose an essay in which, minimally, they had to name the writer of the song, who sang it, the meanings of the lyrics, and finally, what did they learn about the events that had occurred that referred to in the song.

Of course, once you explain the rules, your A+ personality types will start bragging about what they will do with their $100. Let them brag. It can become contagious and get other students to challenge them.

What Makes a Great Teacher?

Explain how you want their paper formatted. I always insisted on them being typed, double-spaced with 12 fonts. Grading would be based on formatting, content, grammar and spelling. What they did not realize and never complained, was that to answer all the questions in construct their essay, would require well over five paragraphs from them. This would be addressed at the end of the contest when I praised everyone who participated and pointed out that they all wrote well over a five-paragraph essay.

I was astonished at their completed assignments. Even my weaker students turned in vastly improved essays. Unfortunately, they did not win any of the "money" prizes, but, on the day that I announced our winners, I had my teaching assistant go out and buy several large pizzas and we had a post-essay contest party. I also gave everyone, including the winners, a "Certificate of Achievement" award that they could take home to their parents and frame.

So, what did I gain from such a contest? Well, I learned that I was now out $225, and would have a nice bill waiting for me after I took all the winners out to dinner. But more importantly, my students had fun learning. They learned that like life, there will be winners and losers. The weaker students realized that I sincerely appreciated their efforts and awarded them instantly with pizza and a Certificate of Achievement. They learned that I was "for real," and sincerely concerned for their success.

I also liked to play "Colombo" in my classroom. Colombo, played by the late actor, Peter Falk, was an unassuming police homicide detective of Italian descent, whose clothes were disheveled and whose trademarks include wearing a rumpled, beige raincoat over his suit, and smoking a cigar. He is consistently underestimated by his suspects who, while initially reassured and distracted by his circumstantial speech, **become**s increasingly annoyed by his pestering behavior. Despite his unassuming appearance and apparent absentmindedness, he is extremely intelligent and shrewdly solves all his cases.

No, I did not wear a dumpy trench coat, nor did I smoke a cigar, but I did, at times, play apparent absentmindedness in front of my class. Why? To draw out participation.

For example: I start out solving an Algebra problem (whatever discipline you want to use) and deliberately either forget a step or make a calculation error, waiting for my students to quickly correct me. Having your students "teach" you is a powerful way of getting them to learn.

Great Teachers Communicate Frequently with Parents

Do not become disheartened when dealing with many of your at-risk students' parents. The old adage of *"the apple doesn't fall far from the tree,"* will be exhibited time and again. Keep in the back of your mind, that in many cases, the reason some at-risk students are at-risk, is due to their parents and lack of having positive role models. The title of one of my future books will be entitled *"It's the Parents Stupid!"* in which I can reminisce about my interactions with several at-risk parents where I concluded that some parents should never have had kids.

Since you will probably have a whole class of at-risk kids in a continuation high school, and for sure, in locked down facilities, you will have some occasions of meeting with your students' parents. These meetings most likely will be parent-teacher conferences, IEP meetings, or behavioral meetings for various transgressions of your students. You could also find yourself in probation hearings in front of a Superior Court judge.

Remember, the key to these meetings is to keep an accurate record of what transpired. I would always write personal notes about these meetings in a locked drawer until the time I felt I no longer needed them. Many times, these notes, containing exact quotes from parents, helped me take on unruly adults, who tried to intimidate me on behalf of their son or daughter.

Sadly, many of my at-risk students had one or both parents either in prison or on parole. They will state to you that they are great role models and will support all your suggestions. More than likely, this will not happen. I had one former student visit me one day after school, stating that he just got out of jail. He said that he and his father watched the Super Bowl together and that they both had their feet up on a table displaying ankle monitors they were both sporting. Another student bragged to his classmates, that his dad recently got sentenced to Pelican Bay prison, and someday he hoped to be incarcerated there also.

My advice is not giving up. Some parents who have served time in prison, will strive to make sure that their son or daughter will not go down the same path that they did. One parent (single mother) was so proud of her daughter's grades in my class, that she promised that she would give up cocaine. "Sure," I thought. Several weeks later, in a writing exercise, this student confided in me that things were now much better at home. Her mom helps her with assignments. They go places together, and she said her mom did not use drugs or alcohol anymore.

Another illustration about parents of at-risk kids. By the time many of the students came to my site, they had major disciplinary problems ranging from truancy, drug and alcohol abuse, criminal activity, assault on parents and teachers – it ran the gamete. Yet, during first day orientation, the student would come in with their parent(s) texting on their new iPhone their parents had just got for them. They had been suspended or expelled from their traditional school; some served time in juvenile hall, yet here they were, entering an alternative education site, with a new $500 plus smartphone given to them as a gift. What had they done to earn this gift? They got kicked out of school, shown disrespect for authority figures, assaulted teachers, possibly placed on probation, so they were rewarded with a new phone.

To summarize, always write personal notes at the end of the day. So many things can happen quickly in a classroom filled with at-risk students that you will forget the many events that will unfold. Before I forget, if you are a male alternative education teacher, never be in a room with a single female alone. First, it eliminates any chance for something innocent to be misconstrued. Secondly, many if not most, of your extreme at-risk kids, yearn for a father or mother figure. At the academy, my teaching assistant was called "mom" and I was referred by them as "dad." We became a family together. But sadly, some had been molested at home by a relative and many still suffered psychological trauma due to those events. It is just good practice to not be in a room solo, nor should you touch a student. There will be times when you might give a "high five" in front of the class. That is ok. But many students are so needy for affection, that they will, without thinking, come up to you and give you a big hug. What I always tried to do, was quickly place my hands in my pockets so that I could not return the hug. They got the idea. Remember, they are very impulsive and for many, that is what got them into trouble in the first place.

Finally, you will judge them. It is human nature to judge. You will compare their lives, belief systems, outlook on the world, to your own background. I still do this today, while teaching adult inmates. But, when they asked for my counsel on issues, and I knew that they would not like my response, I would first say, *"with love in my heart,"* and then give them my take on the subject. These five words, said before I spoke, always goes a long way into how they will later respond. Try it.

"Ask yourself if what you are doing today is getting you closer to where you want to be tomorrow."

"DISCIPLINE IS NOT A DIRTY WORD"

Many educators over the years, have used this phrase, or something similar, to describe their philosophy on classroom management. I prefer to refer to the famous quote of former principal Joe Clark, when he said, "Discipline is not an enemy of enthusiasm."

Always remember that your at-risk students probably come from dysfunctional families where there is no real role model. That does not mean that their parents are bad, it could mean that due to economic conditions, both parents must work, and their child is left unsupervised. They may come from single parent families, and once again, there is a lack of supervision.

Most students, when you talk about discipline, automatically equate it with punishment. And sadly, in many of their homes, punishment is a daily or hourly event, including corporal punishment. In other homes of at-risk youth, as I previously stated, in an attempt to discipline, parents reward their children with presents as a bribe. This is just rewarding bad

"Discipline Is Not a Dirty Word"

behavior. Their children are not being held accountable nor responsible for their actions.

In the academy, for over two and half years, discipline was embedded into the program. Coming from a law enforcement career, and working in partnership with the U.S. Army, our cadets saw discipline in a more positive connotation. It was pointed out to our cadets, that the reason law enforcement and the military stresses discipline is because these services know that discipline allows their organizations to function efficiently as a team.

Sometimes when I would stress that we had to operate as a team, I would use the game of football to illustrate my point. I would have my class envision that they, as a team, were on the half yard line about to score the winning touchdown. One and a half feet to go. 18 inches and they would win the game. There were only a few seconds on the clock.

Just before the ball was hiked, one of them jumped offsides. Now, instead of the ball being on the half yard line, we went backward to the 5 ½ yard line, and subsequently, did not score.

Everyone must work as a team. Everyone is held equally responsible. They learned that discipline would help them develop self-control, which many of them lacked.

With the help of army personnel, my students learned leadership and the importance of teamwork. The army would put them in situations, especially during physical training, in which teamwork was the key to accomplishing the stated task.

I firmly believe and demonstrated it in the academy and in the other court and community school's settings, that classroom teachers can use the same principles used in law enforcement and military boot camps, that discipline can help your at-risk students develop self-discipline, self- esteem, as well as respect for their fellow students. This, we showed, even worked with rival gang members in the same classroom.

One of the constants that my cadets refer to in our book *Hitting Rock Bottom*, is how the order, structure, and discipline of the academy, was the exact chemistry they needed to succeed. They realized that when left up to them, they consistently made bad choices, but with strong adult guidance displayed by the teaching staff and army personnel, they could adopt the concept of accountability and responsibility.

Trust me that when you run your classroom in a disciplinary fashion stressing order, structure and discipline, you students will flourish. They do not have to worry about being called out, bullied, criticized, or disrespected. They are all in it together as a family, and as a family, we might sometimes get upset with each other, but we remain a family none the less.

So how do you set up the ground rules in your classroom? It all starts day one when you meet your students for the first time. Psychologists and others, state that you are judged by others in the first seven-seconds of introduction, but a series of experiments

"Discipline Is Not a Dirty Word"

by Princeton psychologists Janine Willis and Alexander Todorov reveal that all it takes is a tenth of a second, not seven seconds, to form an impression of a stranger from their face, and that longer exposures don't significantly alter those impressions. (www.psychologicalscience.org/observer/how-many-seconds-to-a-first-impression)

Forget whatever figure you may have heard because your at-risk student will only need a split second to see if you have your act together and spot any weakness you might have that they can probe. That is not meant to intimidate you, but that is a fact. They are experts in judging people. Many have had to do so for a long time, living on the street and getting by. They will look at how you dress, do your hair, your body language, your voice, how you walk, how you interact with their fellow students. And they are doing this in a blink of an eye.

I have found that at-risk students are naturally curious and want to learn, but they have more fears than traditional students who want to go to school and have experienced earning good grades. Their track record so far has been poor, mainly due to their lack of attendance and having a "don't give-a-damn" attitude. Now they realize that they are in an alternative education setting and this might be their last chance of getting their act together. Due to this, their enthusiasm may wane. They fear to continue to earn failing grades, not being popular, being picked on by bullies. In other words, they fear to continue down the spiral path that they are currently on.

While they are in your classroom, they may not have all their concentration on the material at hand. Perhaps their parents are divorcing, or worst, in jail. They too may be facing abandonment, incarceration, and dependency on alcohol or drugs. If they are into gangs or being intimated into joining one, they may worry about being jumped or becoming a victim of a drive-by shooting.

We could speculate for days about the fears your at-risk students may bring into your classroom. You may want to, but you cannot address all their fears. Try not to get involved in the drama they are living. I know it is easier said than done because we want them to become successful, but as it was pointed out to me by a close friend and colleague, you cannot save all of them.

Taking this all under consideration, what can you do? Lets' start with reducing the fears of some of your students. Create in your classroom a safe sanctuary where your students can feel safe and protected. They will know what you expect from them and what you will not tolerate from their fellow students. By reducing their fears, you open the door to their education.

In my first book, *Towards the Integration of Police Psychology Techniques to Combat Juvenile Delinquency in K-12 Classrooms."* I alluded to the fact that our teaching colleges spend a limited amount of time focused on classroom management techniques. This

"Discipline Is Not a Dirty Word"

leads to many new teachers leaving the profession as an alarming rate, and I predict, it will only get worst since we seem, as a society, to be moving away from the concepts of accountability and responsibility.

My suggestion is starting the first few days, of school, you act "mean." By that I mean, act professional, but project an image of yourself as a teacher who will not tolerate any misbehaving. Act like you have a chip on your shoulder. Go over your expectations and if you must, because of your administrator, discuss posted classroom rules. Emphasis the consequences of rule violations as well as the concept of accountability. Be stern, more like a taskmaster. Believe me, you will only have to act this way for a few days. This is during the time they are probing for weaknesses and what you will do if they transgress.

You have now set the boundaries of what you will tolerate. They will try occasionally to probe you, but you have set the tone of your classroom. Occasionally I would pick a day, usually in the morning before I got started with my lesson plan, to become upset and display such in front of my students. This I found, keeps them a little off balanced. However, it prepares them for days they go to work and have a boss that is a little cranky.

I was never afraid to display some of my emotions. It made me look "real" to them. They will spot you if you are "phony," so don't try to con them: just be real. Remember, you are trying to act as a positive role model which most of them are lacking, so act in a way in which they perceive you as sincerely caring for them, even when you are having a tough day.

On a few occasions, I have suspended students. Your remaining students will learn of your actions to one of their classmates, and you must repair whatever damage that may have caused with your bonding effort with them. I am always upfront. I explain why the student was suspended without violating any confidentiality issues. Most of the time, the offense was committed in the classroom, so everyone witnessed the event. I think it might be best if I give an example since each teacher, student and event are unique.

My teaching assistant told me that she saw a student enter the boy's bathroom and when he heard her approach, nervously exited the room. I went in and searched and found that someone had pulled the garbage can liner out of the receptacle and replace it haphazardly. I removed the liner and found a plastic baggie of marijuana. I did not remove it, but put the liner back on. I instructed my assistant not to allow anyone any bathroom breaks until break time. Only one person was allowed to use the bathroom at a time, so it was easy for me to go in and check the garbage can after each student used the facility.

Sure enough, the offending student asked to use the bathroom. I gave him permission. He went in, flushed the toilet and then left. I quickly went in and lifted the garbage bag and the marijuana was gone.

I caught up to the student near my assistant's office and asked him to enter. Because he was on probation

"Discipline Is Not a Dirty Word"

and we were a court and community school, he was subject to search. There it is was in his pocket.

The police were called and I suspended him for three days (the maximum days a teacher could suspend at the time.) As soon as the other students saw me enter my assistant's office with the student, most of them knew he was "busted." The police came, cited him, and he left with his parent.

Now to explain it to the class. *"Ladies and gentlemen, once again I have been placed in a position that forces me to take action. Drug contraband is not allowed on campus and I should not even have to bring it up. Unfortunately, someone decided to break the law and now I must discipline him. That is all I am going to say about the matter. If you have questions, you can talk to me at the break or you can contact him at home after school."*

Short, sweet and directly to the point. No gloating or "I got him." In fact, even if he was one of my most irritating students, I acted as if it really hurt my feelings.

The military boot camp academy ran for two and a half years. My students were the most challenging students the county had to offer. They were referred to the Alder Grove Academy from all of the county high schools, junior high schools and continuation schools. Many came from dysfunctional families and low end of the socio-economic ladder. In some cases they were being raised by their grandparents, since both of their parents were incarcerated. Many were on probation, yet I can count the number of students

Gary J. Rose, Ph.D.

I suspended on one hand with a few fingers left over. Why? Because they knew that if they forced my hand, there would be consequences for their action. I had already set the tone with my demeanor I displayed from day one.

"Accept responsibility for your actions. Be accountable for your results. Take ownership of your mistakes."

ACCOUNTABILITY AND RESPONSIBILITY

Lets' start with defining what is juvenile delinquency. I will make several references to social psychology and educational psychology so that you have a firm foundation on what the experts feel cause juvenile delinquency and at-risk students. Juvenile delinquency is generally defined as an accumulation of recorded behavioral issues or criminal behavior among school-age youth, and can also include unexcused absences from school (Office of Juvenile Justice and Delinquency Prevention, 2012). Juvenile delinquency is considered a significant indicator of various educational problems. There are a number of different interconnected issues linked to an increase in a young person's propensity for delinquency, as detailed below.

The first issue is linked to the young person's social setting and the challenges they face therein. Introduced in 1977 by Bronfenbrenner, ecological theory has been used to explain juvenile delinquency. The ecological theory posits that a child's development is influenced by different levels of his or her environment: micro, mezzo, and macro. How the different structures in the environment interact is inextricably linked to how a child functions and performs. A child's development does not occur in a vacuum; a child develops in relation to family, home, school, community, and to society in general. The features of these environments and the interactions that take place within them significantly affect a child's developmental progress. Underlying the ecological perspective are principles such as the person-environment fit, coping, life stressors, and adaptedness (Kelly, Ryan, Altman & Stelzner, 2000).

The social development model provides insight into tracing developmental processes in the life of a child that might predict problem behaviors such as delinquency. It merges three existing theories to explain problem behavior (Brown, et al., 2005): social learning theory (Bandura, 1977), control theory (Matsudo, 1982). The model explains how a child can acquire various experiences in the developmental stages that could lead to pro-social or antisocial behavior (Brown, et al., 2005; Catalano & Hawkins, 1996). The social development model has criminological theory as a foundation and is based on a model of delinquent behavior developed by a number of researchers (Choi, Harachi, Gillmore, & Catalano, 2005). The proponents of the social development mode define antisocial behavior to include "violation of legal codes, including those relative to age" (Catalano, Oxford, Hanichi, Abbott, & Haggerty, 1999.) Truancy falls under this definition. It is possible to predict risk factors (behavioral and situational) by incorporating the main concepts of the social development model with what delinquency researchers have found.

Social learning theory (Bandura, 1977; Bandura, 1963) indicates how children learn behavioral patterns by interacting with many socializing agents. Children retain, maintain, or extinguish behaviors depending on the feedback they receive. They adopt rewarded behaviors, maintain reinforced behaviors, and extinguish punished behaviors. They acquire cognitive and socio-emotional skills which enable them to make decisions regarding whether or not to adopt certain behaviors. Socializing agents play an important role because students look up to them when making decisions about how to behave. The social development model incorporates the social learning theory by suggesting that behaviors developed by students are influenced by the social learning process, and that students acquire cognitive and socio-emotional sills through the system of rewards, punishments, and reinforcements.

Finally, differential association theory (Matsueda, 1982) similarly posits that behavior is learned through interaction with other people – like other at-risk students. Children behave in conformity with the norms and values of any group with which they frequently associate. Family, schools, and communities have a significant role in guiding students towards those pathways by developing in them pro-social or antisocial beliefs (Choi, Harachi, Gillmore &

Catalano, 2005). In other words, a youth can acquire either pro-social or antisocial behavior depending on the type of feedback he or she receives.

Investigating the problem with delinquency and at-risk youth can be made from an ecological perspective because the perspective harbors the view that behavior cannot be understood fully without context (Kelly, 1979). Habitually delinquent students, who refuse to go to school, or, once there, refuse to perform as required, present a myriad of factors as demonstrated by a number of studies. For instance, Reid (2005) developed a general profile of the habitually delinquent student and identified key factors that influence such behavior. Older students, less popular students and bullying victims (Gastic, 2008) were more likely to be delinquent. Other factors include peer pressure not to attend school, disorganized classroom and school environments, lack of parental involvement, and lower socio-economic status of the community. All are strong predictors of delinquency (Fantuzzo, Grim, & Hazan, 2005). Moreover, researchers have found that habitually absent students receive lower academic achievement rates, lower IQ scores, and lower grades (Henry, 2007).

Understanding how paradigms create a framework for social change within schools provides a means by which to address students' delinquent behavior and sets the foundation from which you, as at-risk teachers, can operate from.

But you ask, what can I do about the overarching reasons that help form juvenile delinquency in some

Gary J. Rose, Ph.D.

of our youth? You have taken the first step by now having an understanding of the various theories explaining how juvenile delinquency is developed. You as a teacher can attack some of these problems in the following ways:
1. Develop a collaboration effort with law enforcement officers, educators, students, parents and perhaps, even the community they come from to offer educational support for the classroom and identify student delinquency and psychological issues before they become difficult to manage.
2. Help students resist the many pressures that tempt them to experiment with alcohol or drugs, to ignore school ignore school priorities, or to engage in violence.
3. Improve the quality of life for school students through peer group influences and teacher mentoring.
4. Transform the culture of your classroom and school, thereby providing your students with an environment containing opportunities for social-emotional learning as well as for learning traditional academic subjects.

A successful teacher will incorporate these goals into your curriculum in topical areas such as health, science, social studies, language arts, and other appropriate areas. You should strive for the establishment of peer support programs, even if it is limited to your own classroom. Peer support programs are, on a macro scale, educational organizations committed to improving the quality of life for school students through peer-group influences. The goals include helping primary and secondary school students develop self-esteem (more on that later) and self-awareness, resist peer group pressure, adjust to a new school, and promoted responsibility, accountability, self-confidence, and leadership qualities. Implement these goals in a micro setting such as your classroom.

In our military school, as well as my next assignment in a court and community school, I used peer pressure to bring the class together. I previously cited how a football team, needing to score from the 18" line, lost due to the action of one of their teammates. There is no reason that analogy cannot be used to explain that the action of one student may carry consequences for the other students.

For some of you, it may not be easy initially to instill this behavior in your students, but by demonstrating a zero-tolerance attitude regarding classroom management, students will slowly learn to develop it. Here are some ideas to achieve student accountability in your classroom:

Define Student Accountability

Define for your students the first day of class, the definition of student accountability? Few students understand the need to take responsibility for their actions. At home they pretty much did what they want at home due to lack of proper role models. Therefore, it is essential that you frame rules at the beginning of the year on the actions that are acceptable and unacceptable in the classroom and the consequences for any violations. Unacceptable behavior should have a prescribed consequence that should be followed closely. The student then decides whether he/she performs the acceptable/ unacceptable task. Understanding this crucial concept will help students take responsibility for their actions. Later I will review some of the latest behavioral practices being used in many school districts. Some have promise, but many do not help control classroom disruptions.

Rules are Rules

Be firm with your rules. It is often observed that leniency only encourages students to break rules, and I guarantee you that at-risk students love the challenge of seeing your reaction if a rule is violated. You must "nip it in the bud." Watch out for being accused of having a favorite student. When a teacher bends the rules for someone in class, others will expect the same treatment. Failure to comply will lead to complaints of favoritism that adversely affect the dynamics of the class. Establish your rules and do not be afraid of giving out discipline. It is a good way to instill accountability in your students. Remember one of my favorite quotes by Principal Joe Clark, "*Discipline is not an enemy of enthusiasm.*"

Create a Positive Environment in Your Classroom

Be positive, non-judgmental and supportive to the students. When I had to give out discipline, I never let it interfere with my classroom agenda for the day. In other words, I acted like it was just a small inconvenience, and now that it is over, onward we will go. Since your students are trying to change their behavior, there may be slip ups initially. Remind the student that every action has a consequence and that it was their choice to face the punishment. You may also have a group system in which students remind and support each other.

Teacher-Student-Parent

Inform parents of the game plan. At times, incorrect or imprecise information is conveyed to the parents. To prevent this and generalize student accountability even outside the class environment, parents should be kept in the loop. If a student misbehaves or fails to turn in the work on time, you can ask the child to call and inform the parents in your presence. Such practices will reduce the incidence of mistakes from occurring and increase the practice of taking responsibility.

Follow a plan

Help your students develop a plan to achieve their goals. Instruct them to draw a triangle. At the tip of the triangle, write the goal that needs to be achieved (i.e. improving performance, submitting assignments on time). On the base, write down the steps necessary to achieve the goals. This gives them the opportunity to formulate their own goals and strategies. Writing them down serves as a reminder to the students on their committed to their goals and teachers may encourage them to sign the work and get it signed by their parents. A copy of this is maintained by both the staff and parents to help the student achieve his/her goals. After two weeks, teachers and students can review the goals to see how much was attained, discuss whether the goals were realistic, figure out changes to the plan or set new goals. Such practices will help students to be proactive in their learning.

Keep an achievement chart

Another way to instill student accountability is to encourage students to evaluate their own work, performance, and participation in class. Create an achievement chart that records the various activities and behaviors in class (for example, active involvement in class, academic performance in tests, timely submission of assignments, achievement of goals, etc.). This chart is to be scored by the student daily on a three-point scale of 0, 1, and 2 where 2 is good, 1 is average and 0 is bad. At the end of each week, the student adds the score and makes a chart which is a record of their learning. The chart demonstrates how well each student has achieved their objectives of learning and which areas need more work and effort.

Thus, by teaching students to be accountable for their work and take responsibility for maintaining a level of academic performance, we are encouraging them to oversee their own success.

Gary J. Rose, Ph.D.

"Know your stuff. Create something new. Structure your role. Keep the energy going."

HOW TO BE AN EFFECTIVE TEACHER

Think about the awesome power we have as a teacher. We have the ability to create a long-lasting influence with their students. You get to decide what they learn, how much material they will be exposed too, and we determine what social skills they need to survive in the real world. We have even more power while teaching and interacting with incarcerated youth and adults. Consider your influence on these at-risk students and the power you have to promote positive results in not only their academic achievements but other desirable outcomes.

So, what makes an effective teacher? Some educational researchers define teacher effectiveness in terms of a student achievement. Others define it by rating their teacher's performances from student comments, state/federal exam results, and promotional rates of their student population. This might seem somewhat arbitrary but since this seems to be the prevailing "best" practice, how do you determine an effective teacher assigned to a couple of at-risk incarcerated youth and adults?

Labeling students "at-risk" has been used in education for many decades but really gained prominence in 1983 after the publication of a report titled *A Nation at Risk* (National Commission on Excellence in Education). In an earlier chapter I discussed the characteristics of an "at-risk" student and incarcerated juveniles and adults would definitely be at the extreme end of the spectrum. So, in reposing the question, what qualities does a new teacher need to possess to be effective working with this category of students?

First, there is still a debate raging today over how to recruit, select and prepare individuals to become successful teachers. One of the questions is if a teacher's intellectual ability or aptitude parlay to them becoming effective teachers of locked up individuals.

One research study found that one of the key components of an effective teacher is their verbal abilities. This study found that students taught by teachers with greater verbal skills learned more than those taught by teachers with lower verbal abilities (Rowan, Chiang & Miller, 1997; Strauss & Sawyer, 1986). This study found that teachers with better verbal abilities can convey ideas and lessons to students and communicate with them in a clearer manner.

In an excellent book published in 2007 by James H. Stronge (*Qualities of Effective Teachers* – ISBN: 978-1-4166-0461-7) created a checklist of what he considered qualities of an effective teacher. In reviewing his list, I concur that a person teaching incarcerated juveniles and adults must possess these qualities.

One of the first qualities (and there are many) is that of Teacher as a Person. An evaluator (presumably an administrator) would use this checklist and check the appropriate square (rating) of what he/she observed while visiting a teacher under evaluation. In this particular section, the evaluator can make a rating from "ineffective," "apprentice," "professional," and "master." This is followed by a section titled Caring. The evaluator will be looking for the teacher's ability to be an active listener; signs of concern for their students emotional and physical well-being; displays of interest in and concern for the student's lives outside of school; and the creation of a supportive and warm classroom climate.

The list of qualities being evaluated is quite extensive and includes these following headings:
- Shows fairness and respect
- Interacts with students
- Displays enthusiasm
- Motivates
- Dedicated to teaching
- Uses reflective practice
- Strong classroom management
- Displays organizational skills
- Uses disciplinary action when needed
- Knows the importance of instruction
- Time Allocation
- Instructional plans
- Instructional strategies
- Knows content and expectations

- Able to teach complex ideas
- Assigns homework when necessary
- Monitors student progress
- Responds to student needs and abilities

A long list of ideal characteristics that an effective teacher should possess especially when dealing with "at-risk" students. To summarize, an effective teacher must be prepared at the beginning of their career to be effective – to be the best. All effective teachers are discoverers. They are constantly on the lookout for updated material, better methodologies, better ways to not only entertain but educate their students.

They must establish, maintain, and manage by assessing, diagnosing the learning styles that will work best with the majority of students in their classroom population. Rarely will a teacher of "at-risk" incarcerated juveniles and adults have a classroom with the same grade level and/or academic abilities. You will have a mixed bag of learners and must quickly access where the middle road is and teach to that group. This may create some extra work for you when your high-end learners complete your assignment before the rest of the class, necessitating you to make up some more challenging material (the same for those struggling with the material) for them to work.

An effective teacher must be organized not only in time management but having a fallback position for those days when you cannot present the material you had planned to use. In tandem you must communicate your expectations and plan your instructions accordingly.

Besides subject mastery, an effective teacher must present their curriculum in an engaging fashion showing relevance to the real-world to your incarcerated population. I have worked with many intelligent teachers who were masters of their content subjects only to fail in the classroom with their students who were not "at-risk". Why? Because they could not bond with their students nor present their material to them in an interesting manner showing how it relates to their future careers and life.

When I mentioned having the ability to diagnosis a student regarding their learning styles, abilities and temperament, this also encompasses having the ability to monitor their progress, identify a student's potential, and therefore meet the needs of your incarcerated students.

To summarize, an effective teacher of incarcerated students (juvenile and adult) must be knowledgeable; highly motivated; thin-skinned; have some real-life experience, patient; quick on their feet; determined; can handle set-backs; have strong classroom management skills; possess not only "book-smarts" but the ability to teach this to their students with enthusiasm; be motivational; have a great attitude; and love being a mentor.

Wow, that is a lot of skills a teacher needs to possess to be effective with incarcerated individuals. Remember, you are entering a highly-specialized field of education that most of your colleagues would never consider as a career move.

The rewards you will receive when your inmates earn their high school diploma or GED, in my opinion, is more satisfying than seeing traditional students who have loving, supportive families and strong role models, do their walk to the tune of Pomp and Circumstance. Your "at-risk" locked up students will have overcome major mistakes in their lives and through your dedication, you have helped them get back on the right track. Many truly want the opportunity to turn their lives around and when they walk up to you with their diploma or GED award and shake hand, stating "I won't let you down," pat yourself on the back, since you helped create a wage earner and productive citizen versus another recidivism statistic.

"Life is not about how many times you fall down. It's about how many times you get back up."

—Jaime Escalante

TEACHING INCARCERATE ADULTS

Teaching incarcerated adults in a quality educational program brings a plethora of challenges simply by the diversity of the various educational levels of the prison/jail population. Many have limited educational backgrounds due to dropping out of high school, spending a considerable amount of time incarcerated as a youth, or coming from countries who place little value on an education.

Data from a 1997 census cited by Regina M. Foley and Jing Gao (*Journal Article – Correctional Education Characteristics of Academic Programs Serving Incarcerated Adult* – Vol.55, No.1, March 2004, pp 6-21) found that the educational levels of inmates in state prisons who completed either the 8th grade of a portion of their elementary school education to be at 14.2%. Only 28.9% of the inmates completed a portion of high school.

Placer School for Adults (Placer County, California) has responded to this need by offering inmates in our two county jails, programs leading to their GED upon successful passing their exams. At the time of this writing, there are a limited number of courses available that would be judged as vocational such as computer skills, resume building, parenting, and other life skill courses.

How effective are these programs offered by many states and counties? According to a RAND study in 2013, correctional education reduces recidivism by 43%. The RAND study also found that prison/jail education programs increased post confinement employment by 13%. This number is exceeded to 28% when vocational training is part of their program.

So, what is it like teaching in juvenile detention facility, a county jail or state prison environment? Get used to massive security checks, doors opening and closing electronically, or having them opened by a correctional officer or deputy. There is the constant clanging of bars, cat-calling by inmates, prisoners being escorted to various locations in the facility and the occasional assaultive inmate who requires more than one correctional officer to be escorted past you. In the back of your head you remember that the jail/prison has a no hostage policy meaning that if you are taken as a hostage, your value is no greater than an inmate taken hostage by another inmate.

Next are the routine disruptions that occur in your classroom with inmates leaving for attorney visits, doctor/nurse appointments or court appearances. You hope that your students will show up promptly, but you never know as an inmate educator, that upon your arrival for work, an incident occurred that has placed the facility on lockdown with your classes being canceled.

There will also be delays due to commissary day in which purchases by your inmates arrive in their cellblock and must be distributed before they can attend your class.

As I stated earlier when discussing having an alternative plan in case something goes wrong, inmate educators must have resilience and be extremely flexible. If you have material that requires two hours to complete, and now you only have your students for 30 minutes, you better be able to improvise. Although the U.S. Marines use these three words, "*Improve, Adapt, Overcome,*" they also apply to the role of an inmate educator.

Don't let these setbacks create stress. You have to roll with the punches so that you don't freeze up or fall apart when your students need you.

Previously I cited studies that noted a reduction in recidivism directly linked to inmate education including vocational programs. When questioning my adult inmates (male and female) as to why they are taking adult education courses, most state that they want to finally improve their lives and end the cycle of freedom-incarceration. They want to think critically and become better students so that they can get a good paying job, provide security for their families, and help their children with their studies.

For teachers willing to teach onsite and inside the walls of a detention facility, prison security requirements impose a military-style of precision. Teachers cannot enter or leave the confines easily. Clearances are required before you can even enter the premises. Once allowed inside the initial first barrier, you can be searched and have your material examined. Some items such as cell phones are generally not allowed and if you forget, they will be taken from you and returned upon your departure.

The clothing you wear will be scrutinized. No clothing is allowed that is too revealing. No clothing is to be worn that mimics that worn by the inmates. No dangling jewelry or open-toed shoes are allowed.

Movement in most detention facilities is controlled and regimented. Don't plan on being able to run your class a little longer since inmates must keep on track with the institution timetable. Classes can be arbitrarily canceled and work assignments and hours changed without notice, so your student's attendance is not reliable.

Whether you agree with the philosophy or not, detention facilities are first and foremost institutions of control and security- not classrooms or schools. With jails and prisons being closed institutions where control is the primary concern and the questioning of authority is not tolerated, it may come as a shock to you if you came from open places of education as operated in our public education programs, colleges and universities.

Gary J. Rose, Ph.D.

Safety has never been an issue for me or my colleagues inside our county jails. When I and my inmate educators are introduced at various get-togethers with traditional teachers, many stated that they could never teach in such as hostile violent environment, especially upon learning that we do not have a correctional officer of deputy in the classroom with us. My answer to them is that teaching is the jail is a lot safer than where they teach since it is a pretty good bet that my students do not have a gun.

Actually, inmates are grateful for you as their instructor since they realize that few educators would even consider being an inmate teacher. There may be bad blood between inmates when they enter your classroom but few act out. As for me, their instructor, most of the inmates would quickly cover my back in someone becomes assaultive towards me.

Placer County jail has approved for many years the combination of classifications in one classroom – of course, they are not co-ed. Most times I have at least two and as many of three different classifications in my classroom without any problems. They understand that if I request their removal, correctional officers would do so immediately.

Never lose sight of why your students were sent to jail/prison. I have had a great number of enthusiastic and grateful inmate students, but in the back of my mind I know that they are doing time for murder, robbery, rape, arson, burglary, drug offenses, and gang affiliation to mention a few. But at the same time, I realize that after they serve their time, they will be re-introduced to society and if I can make a difference in their lives so that they do not reoffend, then I have done my part.

A stereotype of prisoners is that they are a lazy, lying, cheating bunch looking for the next scam, but prisoners are a mixed bunch. Some prisoners do fit that stereotype, but many made bad decisions. They want to rebuild their lives and gain the skills and qualifications needed to succeed once they are released, ultimately finding a good paying job.

Prison can be a very negative environment. The educational areas are usually the best (and sometimes only) places to retreat from the depressing realities of jail/prison. As such, students tend to be highly motivated.

The most common reasons given by inmates attending inmate education classes were desires to:
- Open and operate a business.
- Get a better job than manual labor.
- Acquire a higher level of education and skills.
- Strengthen their chances of success after release.
- Make something positive out of the negative prison/jail experience.
- Participate in an affordable program.

(Winterfield et al., 2009)

Many realize that skipping or dropping out of high school and making bad choices led them to confinement, but with education, they can contribute to the well-being of their families.

Gary J. Rose, Ph.D.

The Adult Inmate Learner

Adults have more varied and extensive experiences than children and that's what sets them apart. The quality of experiences for adults are different than those of children. This characteristic that sets adults apart from younger learners is the vast wealth of experience that they have accumulated over the years. While they may have limited experience with the topic you are teaching, they nonetheless can often make connections from past experiences in order to help them learn new material.

By using the learners' experience as a way to break the ice with a new group start your bonding with them. Get discussions going about their previous experiences and even consider using an activity that will allow them to share their experiences. This allows learners a chance to draw from their experiences and help put a "real life" perspective on the topic you are teaching and leads to engagement.

The decisions you make about how you will teach should be based on whether you are trying to change attitudes and values, skills and performance, or knowledge and factual information.

Your inmate students know why they are there in your classroom. Their only motivation might simply be to earn early release credits but I still hold them accountable for completing the work my GED students work on. The adult and non-traditional students who find success have a goal they are working toward - a goal that is their own. They aren't there for parents or spouses or bosses or society. They are there because they want something more and they have determined that higher education is the only way they are going to get it.

Most inmate students have a strong support network (although sometimes it is just you, their teacher). The successful adult student has at least one other person to lean upon. This might be a parent or an in-law, a best friend or a spouse, but it could also be a child or a fellow student. Regardless of the relationship, this support network is critical to the successful graduate's ability to persevere.

I had one Latino student who told me his primary motivation was to prove to his daughter that he would turn his life around and his first step would be earning his GED while doing his time in jail. On the day he passed his final exam and earned his GED, he called his daughter at 5 AM and after telling her a fib that he got into a fight and would have to do more time, told her that he now holds a GED. She told him how proud she was of him and realizing that her father was not happy with her current boyfriend, told him that because of his success, she was dropping the individual a would go back to college.

The inmate student believes in their ability to do the work. I tell them upfront that I will teach them everything they need to know to pass the GED math and science exam, all they need to do is pay attention and practice, practice, practice. Everyone questions themselves at one point or another, but I have learned that those students who achieve his/her goals have perfected the art of positive self-talk. This self-talk, the ability to see themselves as prevailing, persevering and ultimately, earning their GED, is a key element in getting their self-esteem back.

I constantly remind them to stay focus and that I only have six weeks to prepare them for a math and science exam that expects them to know what a person with 12 years of high is supposed to have mastered. They must keep their eyes on the prize, no matter how far away it is. I tell them to think of all the other inmates who studied for their GED exams and passed and ask them how they will feel once they earn theirs.

They know how to advocate for themselves. Sometimes you have to stand up to them if they become too adamant about what they want to do in class that differs from your style. Just remind them that all teachers teach differently and with the success rate you have, they might want to give it some time to see if they are learning what they need for the exams.

They understand what's at stake and they use that to motivate themselves. Most adult students have myriad competing needs they must juggle in order to be successful, all of which can seem insurmountable. The victorious student sees these "competing needs" as reminders of what is at stake, and they allow themselves to be inspired to keep working hard in order to achieve their goals. I know two nursing students who are also new parents. Each of them - one male and one female - feel a twinge of guilt when they think of all the time they have missed watching their babies' first years, but they remind themselves that all this time will be worth it in the end, when they are able to provide for their families and be there for the memories to come.

They understand that 90% of success is showing up, day after day. In our jail setting, that is four days a week for three and a half hours a day for six weeks. This may be the biggest asset of all successful adult students. Going to school is hard. It is exhausting. It forces sacrifices most never imagined. It is all too easy to drop classes, refuse to attend and sleep in, and ultimately, to drop out altogether. Indeed, the numbers show that most adult students do just that. But those who succeed keep showing up. They take their classes, looking forward to more classes they can addend after earning the GED. They feel they are on a roll and desire to take other related courses like computer skills, more writing courses and even parenting courses. Yes, there are those inmates that are taking their "refresher" courses simply to get out of their cellblock (tank) and earn six days off their sentence.

Many see themselves as survivors. There is a contingent of people who believe they are victims of a crazy, chaotic world. They are totally innocent of their charges and the DA is setting them up. The successful incarcerated adult student sees him/herself as a survivor. These students use their self-talk and their long-term goal thinking to persevere through a bad teacher, boring cell time, or a frustrating class whose topic does not interest them. They don't waste time blaming others for the things in their lives that slow them down. Rather, they seek ways through the negativity. A survivor problem-solves and troubleshoots. S/he sees setbacks as opportunities. S/he persists, even when all seems lost. These students are the ones who make it through to the end.

Most of the incarcerated inmates I have taught are grateful for the opportunity. Simply stated: people who take the time to feel grateful are more likely to be happy. The adult incarcerated student I've met over the years who have made it to graduation, all share a similar desire to see the world as a good place, waiting for their contribution. It's easy to envision oneself accomplishing anything when one perceives the world as a partner in the process. Students who take the time to be thankful find the energy and the strength to persist in their studies. Gratitude engenders a sense of hope, which is all you need when you are working toward a goal and life threatens to get in the way.

Below are portions of a handbook issued to new inmate educators from the West Virginia Adult Ed Program Office which I feel sums up what you need to do and avoid to be a successful as an inmate educator. These same "dos" and "don't" apply to teaching incarcerated "at-risk" youth.

Adult Education (Adult Ed) Program Office of Adult Education and Workforce Development West Virginia Department of Education Recommendations for Inmate Educators

Do:
- Be firm but fair.
- Be consistent.
- Be objective.
- Demonstrate self-confidence.
- Exhibit a positive attitude toward inmates.
- Suggest rather than order.
- Avoid favoritism.
- Look after the interests of your students.
- Instruct and counsel.
- Recognize change.

Don't:
- Don't strive to be popular among inmates.
- Don't exhibit prejudice.
- Don't discuss other inmates.
- Don't become overly familiar with inmates.
- Don't fear certain inmates.
- Don't demonstrate indifference toward inmates.

Be Firm but fair: Using many of the techniques taught to me as a hostage negotiator, you learn that some adult inmates will try to establish themselves as the Alpha male/female in your class. One strategy they will use is to confront you in a conversation to see if they can get you to back down, thus earning points with their fellow inmates. A teacher of "at-risk incarcerated adults and even their juvenile counterparts want to test you from day one to see what you will accept. In other words, how far can they get without crossing the line and possibly getting kicked out of class or receive consequences from the custodial staff? Remember if your antagonist can upset you, h/she owns you at some level. You must learn how to talk with inmates in such a way that neither of you loses face. Related to this is your use of empathy which I will cover more later.

When an inmate attempts to verbal attack you, remain under emotional control during the disagreement. Maintain professionalism at all cost. Remember, all individuals want to be treated with respect and dignity and this is a very important aspect of an inmate's life in confinement.

Inmates would rather, like most people, be asked politely to do something versus being told to do something. In a detention facility, correctional staff do not have the luxury to be polite and must, due to safety concerns and logistics, order action versus requesting it. Therefore, if you practice asking versus ordering in your classroom, your inmate population will feel a positive change in their environment even for the short time you are together.

Most inmates want a second chance to make up for the mistakes that resulted in their present circumstance. As previously stated, they recognize that you are the person who can help them turn their lives around so most will comply with all your requests.

I was taught in hostage negotiation training that a negotiator must speak "tactically" in order to gain compliance, develop cooperation, and work on a crisis collaboratively. This means having the ability to speak with your inmates without causing or escalating a conflict. You do this by praising without sounding manipulative. You use persuasion to generate voluntary compliance. This is really the heart of hostage negotiations and it works extremely well in a detention facility.

But all of this starts with your mere presence - your representation as an authority figure.

When I walk into the jail, I am always dressed in a suit and tie. My shoes are shined and walking with my briefcase, I try to carry an aura of confidence and strength. I call this command presence. I wear my suit to convey to my inmates that I take my job as their teacher seriously as well as acting as a positive role model for them. I always maintain eye contact while speaking to them. This exudes credibility and an aura of power. I inform them that I represent the Placer School for Adults and I am extremely excited in helping them earn their GED. I outline the course material, my curriculum, and then tell them what they can expect from me – my promise. By this stage I can pretty much determine how many of them have already bought into my program at which time I explain what I expect from them – their attention, focus, cooperation and work on assignments. The goal, getting them to pass the math and science examinations of the GED. In addition, you should treat each inmate the same with dignity and respect. Always act professionally. The inmates will take you more seriously if you do so.

You must become a mediator. The ability to redirect inappropriate behavior when displayed by an inmate. Don't make it confrontational. You may even make a joke about something else taking the attention off them. Here is an example I witnessed by my field training officer when I was a rookie patrol officer.

We responded to a husband and wife family disturbance. My training officer had been there many times before. When we arrived, we could hear screaming from both a male and female behind a closed front door. We then heard what sounded like an object being broken and used that as our invitation into the house. The male and female glanced at us from their location in the kitchen but continued their verbal assaults on each other. I am sure my eyes were wide open expecting a possible fight between us and at least one of them. I took what I felt was a tactical position in case things escalated but witnessed my training officer walk up to the kitchen counter and pick up a newspaper. The three of us (male and female combatants and I) watched my training officer unfold the newspaper and began looking at the want ads. The two continued to throwing insults at each other, but still occasionally glanced at my training officer. During one of their verbal joustings, my field officer said out loud, "Oh my God, a 1967 Malibu SS, cherry condition. Can I use your phone?" Both of the combatants stopped and did not know what to say. He said, "I'm sorry, but I have been looking for a 1967 Malibu SS and I really want to call and see if it is still available." The male turned his attention to my training officer and said: "no, you cannot use our phone." The female joined in and said, "use your own phone," and then turned, took her car keys and left the house. We said our goodbyes to the male and left. What did I just observe and why did it work?

My field training officer used a form of mediation. He deflected the heated conversation onto him and threw them off balance by picking up the newspaper and then asking permission to use their phone.

Can this tactic work in a detention facility? Absolutely. On one incident after our week-long Thanksgiving break, I returned to the jail where I found two inmates extremely talkative and what I term "squirrely". After asking them to please be quiet so that I can continue to present the new math concepts under discussion, they returned to their cross-talking. Finally, I reached into my briefcase on my desk and pulled out my Wall Street Journal and set down and began reading it. After a few seconds I said, "Damn, I need to get home and execute a stock trade as soon as possible. I'm missing out of making some serious money." They got the message without me saying a word to them. I conveyed to them that their time is just as important as mine.

Constantly find the time to explain the relevance of your teaching topic to the goal that you want to achieve. For me, apart from those inmates attending as "refresher" students, the goal is preparation for successfully passing their GED exams. But I also had to make it relevant for my non-GED inmates. With the males, I found that many want to be mechanics, welders, pipefitters, HVAC mechanic, electricians, and other trades. When I told them that many of these trades require an entrance exam to join be considered for employment of joining their union, I got their attention. I actually address this on the second day of class by bringing in a multiple page document listing all of the trade jobs available in the United States and the entry requirements. This article also lists the approximate salaries for each position which is of great interest to my inmates.

To be a successful teacher of "at-risk" incarcerated adults, you must be a good persuader. You must learn how to read your inmates and the various situations you find yourself in with them. After approximately five weeks, I know which of my GED inmates are ready for recommendation to our testing facilitator to take their exams. The hard part is to notify an inmate that h/she is not ready to take the tests. The wrong approach is to simply go up to the individual in front of the rest of the class and say, "You are not ready. See you again in six weeks." You have now disrespected them and even worse, did it in front of their peers. All hell could break loose due to this one error.

Instead, you must diffuse the situation and put yourself into the role of the inmate who for some reason, just cannot get it. I will call them aside out of the ears of the rest of the class and already have in my hand their pre-test showing their failings. I already have a look on my face displaying empathy and sadness. Without saying a word, most inmates will say something like, "I didn't do very well did I?" I respond by highlighting all of the areas h/she were able to answer successfully and congratulate them on their competence. Then I quickly point to their deficiencies and have a book that highlights those areas that they can concentrate on so that they can pass the exam the next time. Most are extremely happy that I have taken the time to point out their strong command of various math problems and they seem earnest in concentrating on those areas of weaknesses.

I had one male inmate student who, after his six weeks with me, and unsuccessful in passing his math exam, was transferred down to our main jail located in another part of the country. Having so many inmate students that come and go every six weeks, not to mention my online graduate students from the university, there are very few students who names I can recall. That said, one day our testing facilitator send me a text that this male inmate specifically requested that she notify me that he passed his GED math exam and thanked me for helping him achieve his goal. This is the power of persuasion in action versus what could have been an ugly verbal confrontation in the classroom.

An inmate educator must have a perspective. Simply stated, this is the way you see things, your point of view, based on your knowledge, your understanding of a situation, your background, and your experience. I share my perspective with all my students the first day of class. In all the years teaching incarcerated "at-risk" juveniles and adults, the fact that I was a retired police sergeant never caused a problem in my classes. Most are taken by surprise that a former police sergeant would now come into a detention facility and give up some of their time teaching inmates how to turn their lives around.

Related to perspective is subject mastery. The more thoroughly you know your subject matter, the more powerful you will present it. There is no substitute for knowing what you want to say, how you want to say it, and this only comes with practice and experience, plus the love of the subject matter.

Recently, my former supervisor told me that since I did not have any GED math or science students in my class, to go ahead and teach whatever subject I wanted too for the six weeks. He knew that having a doctorate in psychology, that I would choose this subject. The inmates were ecstatic about attending what in essence was a six-week college like course in Social Psychology. They could feel my dedication and level of expertise in the subject matter and soon they began asking Placer School for Adults to offer the course as another elective. Your perspective and enthusiasm is easily read by incarcerated adults and many feed off of it. Many told me they told their loved ones during visitation hours that they were taking a college level psychology class. They had a newfound self-esteem and I turned that around on them by saying after they completed their exams, that they demonstrated to themselves that they can do college level work.

You must know your audience. Yes, they are criminals, some waiting for their day in court, others waiting for sentencing. But this is the group as a whole. Individually, each has a story to be told. The males are trying to project and receive respect and to a lesser degree, so do the female inmates. In my second book, *Hitting Rock Bottom,* there is a section titled Final Warning in which many of the male and female inmates I was teaching asked if they could have their stories published with the same purpose in mind as my cadets – hopes of turning someone else's life around. The commonality of their stories was coming from broken homes, getting addicted to drugs and or alcohol, running with the wrong crowd and making too many mistakes. So, to make them accept me, I inform them that counting all the time I spent as a teacher at our juvenile detention facility and in the county's two jails, I have been "locked" up for over 25 years. I then add the fact that I do get to go home, but that I have also become accustomed to clanging electronic doors, smells of the institutions, and being order and searched by the correctional staff. Why did I do this? Because I was attempting to be a "real" person who, although I got to return to my home, have experienced some of the "niceties" of the jails. That powerful word empathy comes into play. Put yourself into their shoes.

Your voice in the classroom with incarcerated juveniles and adults is very important. Fortunately for me, I have a strong deep voice that I can raise several octaves when I get upset. I use this ability as part of my command presence in front of my students. I don't bad mouth them but instead can raise my voice in such a way that I drown out those that have the desire to speak when I am speaking and once I get them quiet, carry on. Combine the use of your verbal skills with your command presence. In essence, you should become an actor and entertain will teaching to keep their attention. You will know you have them in the palms of your hands when you begin walking from one side of the room to the other constantly scan their faces to establish eye contact.

It is extremely important that you are organized, that you know your purpose and plan for what you are going to teach. Inform your students of your "bottom line." In my current assignment, that is teaching GED inmates what they need to know to pass their exams. I am surprised when some of my collogues go into a classroom of incarcerated individuals with their planned curriculum and presentation, prepared, with knowledge of their audience, with great voice inflection, only realize later, that they did not achieve their purpose. My GED inmates know from day one what my purpose is – to help them pass their exams. On the day of their exams, I request all of them to have the test facilitator text me that they passed. This reinforced in their minds what my purpose is.

Along with command presence comes ethical presence. I make sure my inmates understand in effect that I am working with them and all that they have to do is fall my lead. I keep my professional face in front of them. When they start having problems with certain math concepts, I show my concern and quickly come up with ways that might help their comprehension.

Another good technique to use with your incarcerated students is paraphrasing. Don't interrupt them when they start to complain that they "just don't get it." Let them vent their frustration. Then, paraphrase what they just told you using what is called "I messages." For example, "I understand Jim that inequalities might be hard to understand the first time you deal with them. Let's see if I can explain it another way." I used paraphrasing and empathy. He sees me as genuinely caring about his learning and sees that I am getting right in there with him so he can comprehend.

Finally, always remember to praise your students. I constantly thank my students at the end of the three hours of instruction how much I appreciate them for staying focus realizing that studying math that long can be tedious. We are not allowed to bring in any type of treats to the jail, so my form of reward, if they stayed focused for the first three or four days, is to show them a movie as my reward for their efforts. They love it. But, I made sure day one, that they realized that they had to earn it. Don't pay attention and do the assigned work, and the movie on Thursdays is gone.

In summary, most prison/jail inmates (and I include incarcerated juveniles) know the importance of education, want to participate in correctional education programs, and are motivated students. Prisoners want to build a better future, and education is often a positive experience.

A stereotype of prisoners is that they are a lazy, lying, cheating bunch looking for the next scam, but prisoners are a mixed bunch. Some prisoners do fit that stereotype, but many made bad decisions. They want to rebuild their lives and earn the skills and qualifications needed to succeed once they are released.

Education, and when offered vocational training areas, are usually the best (and sometimes only) places inmates can retreat from the depressing realities of confinement. As such, students tend to be highly motivated.

Researchers organized focus groups of inmates enrolled in post-secondary education and asked what drew them to those programs (Winterfield, Coggeshall, Burke-Storer, Correa, & Tidd, 2009). The most common reasons given were desires to:

- Open and operate a business.
- Get a better job than manual labor.

- Acquire a higher level of education and skills.
- Strengthen their chances of success after release.
- Make something positive out of the negative prison experience.
- Participate in an affordable program.

(Winterfield et al., 2009)

> *"The mediocre teacher tells.*
> *The good teacher explains. The superior teacher*
> *demonstrates. The great teacher inspires."*
>
> —William Arthur Ward

WHAT TO TEACH

Remember that you will probably not have your at-risk students for a long time. They are very transitory in nature, especially if you are assigned to a locked down facility. In our district, the job of Alternative Education was to help our students return to their traditional schools, or, for those close to graduating, assist them to reach that goal. This sound fairly straight forward, but it is not easy.

In Placer County, alternative education programs come under the jurisdiction of the County Office of Education. A director and her assistant, oversaw six separate sites, with ten teachers, nine teaching assistants, and several special education teachers. The sites stretched from Roseville, Rocklin, Auburn, up to the Lake Tahoe region in California.

Some sites, such as the juvenile detention facility in Auburn, had four teachers and four aids just to handle the layout of the facility. Students were screened by the probation staff regarding their age, sex, the sophistication of their crimes, gang affiliation, and placed in their appropriate housing unit. It was in these housing units, that their education took place. Their "classroom" doubled as their "dayroom" when there were no classes. To envision the layout, there was a top floor and bottom floor of cells (rooms) that housed the wards. Two juveniles per room containing a top and bottom bunk. There were no toilets in these rooms, requiring the ward to press a button, informing the dispatcher, that they needed to use the bathroom.

In the morning, the wards were awakened and after they made their bunks, they would line up for breakfast and either walk down to the cafeteria or eat in their dayroom/classroom. Once that was completed, they would sit in the classroom until their teacher arrived.

Placer County's juvenile detention facility contains three general housing pods. A-C. When the facility first opened, all general housing units were used as classrooms. The older males were in A-unit, older females in B unit, and the younger less sophisticated students were housed in C unit. In addition, there was a maximum-security unit located at the opposite end from general housing. This unit had one room per individual which also contained a bathroom.

My purpose for such a detailed description of the layout of the juvenile detention facility is to describe how different it is when compared to traditional schools. Students do not attend a class and upon hearing a bell, move on to their next one. They come to class, have one teacher who will teach a few subjects; have their breaks, lunch, and end the school day. It is a self-contained classroom. Many alternative education schools are fashioned in the same manner, but yours' may be different.

I rarely saw my colleagues until break time nor had a lot of interaction with their students. I had the older males in A-unit and they were my responsibility. Now, regarding what I taught, I was fortunate to have a great director, who liked the fact that I taught in the A-unit, all the subjects normally taught in a traditional high school. My subjects included; Algebra, U.S./World History, English, Economics and Life Science. Emphasis is on reading, writing, and math. Regardless of the subject matter I taught, I tried to have reading, writing, and math embedded in the lesson plan. Extra credit was given to free reading outside the classroom after a required book report was completed. Exams were held each Friday. This is when I started calling exam day, Pay Day!

The problem I encountered in my unit of older males, was multiple grade levels of $9^{th} - 12^{th}$ graders and varying levels of academic abilities in the same grade. Some 9th graders were prepared to study Algebra II, while others still struggled with fractions. So, I decided to "teach to the middle." In other words, it did not take me long to see at what academic level, most of the wards to handle. Because the student population could change daily, I constantly had to monitor how challenging I could make their

What to Teach

curriculum, or in reverse, how I needed to spend more time on a subject, before moving on.

For example, on many occasions, I would be in the middle of Algebra I, when several wards would either be released or sentenced to a boot camp school. Many of the newly arriving students did not have the background in math to start Algebra mid-term, so I would have to start all over again. When teaching at-risk students, always realize that the old Marine Corp phrase "improvise, adapt, and overcome," really applies to your methodologies and strategies. You should always have a fallback position: more challenging or less challenging material. A plan if your audio-visual equipment fails.

Later, when I was honored with the creation of the Alder Grove Academy (see my book - *Hitting Rock Bottom*), I continued with my teaching style of posting the agenda for the day including all the previously mentioned subjects. This culminated in their weekly exam.

What was taught was generally left up to the individual teacher and not set by our director. Later, when we attempted to establish our Professional Learning Community (more on that in a later chapter), we adopted as our goal, that our students passing the California High School Exit Exam as well as high school graduation or GED.

This caused some teachers to become a little upset in that they wanted to continue to teach what I considered, less challenging fun stuff like art, or

Pictionary, or just showing movies. These teachers felt that we were now too focused on "teaching to the test." What is wrong with this I constantly asked. When you are trying to get your driver's license, you don't study biology do you? No, you study for the test.

My feelings were and still are, if we want our students to pass an exit exam, or show the government how we rate against other states, we had better prepare our students on what they will be tested on. I remember one colleague, whose teaching philosophy and mine were diametrically opposed, always wanted to have her students do art. One day she was very upset because her students did not want to do her art project. I made the statement, "maybe they know it is not going to be on their exit exam." She did not speak to me for a long time but think about it. Many of them are struggling to stay in school. They run with the wrong crowd. Their grades and credit accumulation are terrible, and we are going to spend precious time, not challenging them to get their act together. Sure, there is time for art and other fun activities, but the main thrust of educating our students, including adults, is to see that they can obtain their high school diploma or GED and fellow a pathway leading to their goal (job and income).

Do not misunderstand. I love to offer rewards to my students and have fun, but it is after I know that I have them prepared for their future educational endeavors. After my Friday exam, that was when we celebrated; after they demonstrated that they mastered

What to Teach

the material taught during the week. Did I teach to the test? ABSOLUTELY! When your students know, what is on the line, be it exams to get a good grade or the now repealed high school exit exam, they will rise to the occasion.

Something else I would like to bring up is the old STAR testing regiment. This has been replaced under Common Core, but for most at-risk students, it is a waste of time. "At-risk" students, even more so than traditional students, need to understand "what's in it for them?"

Why should they take a test that went on for 3-4 days, covering math, science, English, etc., when they do not really receive anything in return. Most at-risk students don't care how the State of California rates against Michigan, or Texas, or Idaho.

In Alternative Education, especially inside juvenile hall, we tried various methods to motivate our students to take these exams seriously. One teacher tried to bribe them, by offering a pizza party after the exams. Our results were still dismal. We could all see some students simply go through the motions of penciling in a (B) choices, or those that really wanted to impress us, choosing first (A), then (B) and so on. What did they get at the end? Pizza just like those few who took the tests seriously.

My way was not any better. I told my students that if, while walking around, I saw them really making an effort on the various sections of the exams, I would give them an (A) grade for the day. Screwing around would result in an (F) grade. So, if they were supposed to be working on Algebra problems, and they really gave me their best effort, I gave them an (A) in Algebra for the day. Since they would later factor that into their weekly grade total, it meant something for them. But, most students slacked off or never even showed up for class during testing week; many with the blessing of their parents!

Make whatever subject you chose to teach, or are mandated to teach by my superiors, relevant to your students. Demonstrate to them the importance of learning the new material and how it will impact them either in high school, trade schools, or their adult lives.

For example, after I retired from law enforcement, I eventually became a stockbroker, financial advisor. During a course on Economics, I did not start off teaching them "supply and demand," but how to invest in the stock market. I had a prepared lesson plan on what is a stock, bond, mutual fund, risk and reward and how they, even as juveniles, could invest in the market with the help of their guardians, and become "filthy rich Americans." They always asked for me to leave them my Rolex and the keys to my Corvette upon my death as a joke, but I turned it around on them, by saying that understanding Economics and the stock market, will help them buy their own Rolex later in life. That was my hook. I showed them the relevance of the topic and how it directly applies to their adult life.

What to Teach

In summary, know your subject matter. Review your lesson plans. Is it entertaining? How will you deliver your material? Will you incorporate DVDs, Internet, group activities? Do you have a "hook" in showing your at-risk students the relevance of the subject matter you are going to be teaching? Is your lesson sprinkled with jokes or fun activities? Is it challenging based on the academic ability of your current student body population? Do you have a "fallback" position in case your students do not comprehend the material? What methods will you utilize in determining their mastery of the subject? Do you have enough material in case your "Brainiac's" get through too soon? How will you handle students that struggle with the material?

You will find days when you seem to be hitting on all cylinders. Your students are engaged, having fun, really learning. Try to remember what you did on those days and employ them on those days, where for whatever reason, nothing seems to work. Don't give up and don't be afraid to share your concerns with your students. Ask them why they are having a bad day. You are now showing them that you are for real. You want them to start thinking of themselves as a family, at least while they are in your classroom.

"Sticks and stones may break my bones, but words will never harm me."

TEACHING SOCIAL SKILLS USING MOVIES AND ARTICLES

Defining social skills Social skills are skills that enable a child or teen to interact and communicate (verbally and non-verbally) in a meaningful way with others. Social skills allow for healthy problem-solving, decision making, self-management, and peer relations. Good social skills are critical to successful functioning in life. These skills enable youth to know what to say, how to make good choices, and how to behave in diverse situations. The extent to which children and adolescents possess good social skills can influence their academic performance, behavior, social and family relationships, and involvement in extracurricular activities. Social skills are also linked to the quality of the school environment and school safety.

Every child has his/her own temperament or "natural or inborn manner of thinking, behaving, and/or reacting. Some children enjoy higher levels of social activity while other children prefer less.

However, social competence, or the ability to get along with others, can be learned. This means that social behaviors can be practiced and improved. Children do not need to be the most popular person in their class, but research highlights the protective factors associated with having a close relationship with a peer.

Youth with poor social skills have been shown to:
- Experience difficulties in interpersonal relationships with parents, teachers, and peers,
- Experience lower self-esteem and poorer frustration tolerance,
- Show signs of depression, aggression and anxiety,
- Are more likely to fail to meet teacher expectations,
- Are at increased risk for unfavorable school outcomes, such as poor interactions with teachers, poor academic performance, and high rates of disciplinary problems,
- Are more likely to drop out of school and use drugs and alcohol when older,
- Demonstrate poor academic performance,
- Show a higher incidence of involvement in the criminal justice system as adults.

These traits are normally displayed by "at-risk" juvenile student inmate and unless modified, continue on with the "at-risk" adult inmate student. Unless corrected or addressed, the "at-risk" adult inmate learner will struggle interpreting relevant social cues;

how to consider response option and cannot respond in a pro-social manner.

Social skills interventions that incorporate social and emotional learning skills have proved to be particularly effective in improving students' attitudes towards school, feeling more connected to school, having more positive attitudes towards themselves and others, reducing conduct problems, decreasing emotional distress (e.g., anxiety, depressive symptoms), and significantly improving academic grades (Durlak, Weissberg, Dymnicki, Taylor, & Schellinger, 2011). But, these programs take time to implement and time to see results.

In our Adult Education program, as an inmate teacher, I have six weeks to prepare my students for their rigorous math and science GED exams which does not leave much time to specifically address social skills, so I must incorporate some of them in my curriculum. When I taught the GED Social Studies and Reading Through Language Arts subjects, I had more latitude in my incorporation of life skills, but it is still possible while teaching math and science.

Throughout the years of teaching "at-risk" students, both juvenile and adult, I found an increase in students that were visual learners. Pure lecture and note taking were beyond their capabilities. These students also seemed to struggle with knowing how to identify emotions or interpret body language of other inmates resulting in them making inappropriate decisions.

To accommodate these visual learners, I updated my previous methodologies by incorporating many visual aids such as topic-related movies, PowerPoint presentations and even animated graphics/cartoons. An example would be the use of a cartoon describing how to use the Pythagorean Theorem (*The Pythagorean Theorem,* Allied Video Corporation,

P.O. Box 702618, Tulsa, Oklahoma 74170, (800) 926-5892). At times, I even used movies that my inmates were familiar with so that I could pause and hone in on a specific element I wanted them to remember.

An example would be the use of the Movie *Titanic*. Of course, my inmates love the scene where Rose, partially nude, is being drawn by Jack, but more importantly, was to draw their attention to the background narratives being discussed by individuals such as the captain, weather reports, number of lifeboats available and so on.

Pearl Harbor is another movie that most of my inmates had seen many times, but they only focused on the action and very little on the actual historical events leading up to the disaster such as the Japanese knowing the depth of Pearl Harbor and attaching plywood fins to their torpedoes.

My inmates knew that following nearly every film, there would be a test based on the hidden historical narratives embedded in these films. We were not just going to watch movies and pass the time. If I use a movie the inmates are not as familiar with, then before I even start I explain that they are going to see and talk about a movie.

More importantly than just using films to augment your lectures is to use them as a method of teaching social skills to your inmate (juvenile or adult). Many inmates lack pro-social skills. Employers find that 74% of high school graduates lack adequate social or soft skills vital for entry-level jobs and if you extrapolate, an inmate social skills are even worse since many have negative or anti-social behaviors.

Schools use to teach math, science, language art, reading–the hard skills – in what I call *Old School*. Up to the early 1960s, parents, as well as organized religion, taught children social skills. However, in today's society, many parents live the teaching of social skills to their children's school. In the case of many juvenile "at-risk" students, their family life is dysfunctional without role models for them to mirror. In some cases one or both parents are in prison so the child learns the wrong skills on the street from other "at-risk" children. Most often, these kids lack needed social skills to interact with peers. It is this lack of social skills that often prevents mainstreaming. Children who are rejected for 2-3 years by the time they enter the 2nd grade have a 50% chance of showing antisocial behavior. In contrast, only 9% of kids who have friends develop antisocial behaviors.

Well known developmental psychologist Urie Bronfenbrenner, (the main subject in my doctoral dissertation) said we cannot understand the kids we work with unless we understand the ecology or circle of family, school, and peers. He is directing this statement towards preschoolers and students in secondary school settings, but it applies to an inmate population since something was lacking in their upbringing that resulted in their criminal activity.

Albert Bandura, famous for his experiment using the BoBo doll, developed a social learning map in which he asserted that aggression is acquired via both direct observation, experience and observation of others. To address these problems there needed to be a combination of cognitive-behavioral counter-interventions but, if a child growing up does not have parents to help with this development, should we be surprised that for some individuals, prison is the outcome?

Another thing to think about is what social skill(s) you want to work on. Pick which scenes you want to focus on before you start. As the inmates get better at a particular skill, you can move on to practicing the next skill. Some movies can be used for many different skills.

One of the social skills I like to target is eye contact and is normally the first skill that I work them on. What I explain to the inmates is that where people look tends to be a clue to what they are thinking about. I then look at my watch and quiz them to guess what I am thinking. Many times I included with eye contact, body language interpretation. I would change my facial expressions from happy, sad, mad, furious and surprised and ask them to use my body language as clues to how I was feeling. Sometimes this social skill training exercise took place when I would pause the movie and have the class discuss the feelings or emotions of various characters. So, as you can see, as I work on emotions, I will break the facial expressions down. I will also point out that body language is important to study because we tend to use a lot of body language in our emotions.

Pausing some movies, I will ask the inmate to focus on the emotions being conveyed by a character such as his eyebrows moving up, his arms on his hips, or the fact that he is moving backward which shows that he is scared. As the inmates get better at identifying an emotion, I will switch it and then ask them "how did you know?" I then see if they can break down the emotion telling me things like his eyes are looking down, he has a frown, so he is sad.

I then move on to the psychological causes of emotions. In other words, what caused the emotion they see displayed by an actor on the screen? As the inmates get better at identifying emotions, I begin working on determining why a particular character had that particular emotion. I will pause the movie to show the facial expression, and then have the inmates identify the emotion while stating, in their opinion, what caused the emotion. Everything I have described so far regarding social skills training with films has a tremendous effect on engagement with you students. Over the years I have found that both "at-rlsk" juveniles and adults are not afraid to speak out, but now, using the Socratic method of teaching, they must "defend" their statement(s).

A tough social skill for many "at-risk" students is predicting what is going to happen next. Sometimes this is due to processing problems. Once the inmate has identified the emotion and what caused it, have them make a prediction as to what the character is going to do next. If the inmate has already seen the movie, then it is harder to do this, but still good to talk about so that the inmates get the connection.

One of the fun social skills to teach inmates is how people can change someone's behavior. For some "at-risk" students it is a harder concept to understand. I heard one teacher explain at a conference how she used the movie Shrek with her students ("non-at-risk"). The cartoon character Donkey, is wonderful at getting Shrek mad by his incessant talking. When Shrek first meets Donkey, the teacher stopped during the interactions and talk about the clues that Shrek gave Donkey - that his talking was making him mad. She also points out that Donkey is not a good social thinker because he is not paying attention to Shrek's body language and words. Another good scene she uses is from the film The Incredibles when it is dinner time. There is a lot of great interaction that causes people to get upset. Ice Age also has a great scene where Sid the Sloth makes some very happy rhinos very upset. Of course, it seems that Sid is good at making a lot of people upset.

I have not used any of these films but if it works for you, go for it.

While teaching Social Psychology at the college level where I did have some visual learners, I used the Disney-PIXAR film *Inside Out*, *Major Pain*, as well as *What About Bob*? All three films are excellent social skills training material.

There are some emotions that are more complex, that in order to understand, you have to be able to take the other person's perspective. They are a lot harder to understand because sometimes you also have to listen to tone of the voice cues. Think of some of the films you have seen where a character is very complex. What makes that individual so complex and hard to evaluate? These films are great for inmates to debate as a group.

The previously mentioned teacher also used the film Ice Age with her middle schoolers. She had them focus on the wooly mammoth Manfred who rescues Sid from the rhinos and has a very sarcastic moment. She talks to her children about how sometimes the meaning of what we say can change according to our tone of voice. After pausing, she demonstrates a happy way of saying what Manfred said and then has her students what that part of the film again listening closely to what he says. She points out that it doesn't sound the same. Repeating herself, she then says it again the same way that Manfred said it. She also points out that Manfred rolled his eyes. This is another clue to sarcasm. She told us that one particular child that she did this with, has his eyes opened so big and he was so excited because he finally understood what it meant to be sarcastic. He tried it out on her and everyone he knew for a week.

Once I have covered the basic emotions I point out that emotions are not always the same. An emotion can have different levels of intensity or different meanings. For example, loneliness and grief have different causes and bring different reactions but often get lumped together as sad.

In summary, Social skills are often taught through a combination of large group instruction, small skill groups, and individual social skills instruction. Evidence-based social skills programs will always include direct instruction, modeling, roleplaying the skill, practicing the skill in different settings, and performance feedback. Currently, my colleagues in Adult Education do not have the time or resources presently to present a full-time life skills program together for our "at-risk" adult inmates but I am aware that the Sheriff's department is looking at implementing such a program.

"I never teach my pupils. I only attempt to provide the conditions in which they can learn."

—Albert Einstein

TEACHING MATERIAL/ EXERCISES/VIDEOS ETC.

In this section, I will list and comment on some of the teaching aids I have used over the years teaching both at-risk juveniles and incarcerated adults. Now that I am closer to the end of my career than the beginning, I find myself with a tremendous amount of material I have accumulated over the last 20+ years. My garage is filled with old VHS tapes and DVDs plus literally hundreds of books covering the various curriculums I have taught. Each winter I have plans to get rid of most of this material, but it seems that once I grab a tape, DVD, or book, I think about how I might use it in the future. With many schools doing away with hardbound texts in lieu of computer based material, I will probably have to dispose of most of my material in the city dumps.

Teaching Material/Exercises/Videos etc.

Pick and choose what you feel might be of interest for your students. Most of the material can be found at times on eBay, Amazon, or other sources.

If you recall earlier in this book, I talked about my meeting with the late Jaime Escalante. In our brief discussion at his award gala, he told me that he rarely found one textbook to satisfy the needs of this students. Instead he said, he was constantly looking for new material to keep his curriculum fresh. He also used books for MIT and other colleges and showed his students that the material he was using was in use in colleges and universities to inspire them. Following his advice, I was constantly on the prowl for new material resulting in a garage full of books etc.

My advice is to continue searching for material other teachers have found successful and are willing to share. I would not have the abundance of material I have accumulated if the Internet was around 20 years ago. There are now hundreds of sites, if not thousands, in which teachers share their material as well as sites offering material for a fee.

Our district had a policy that if we were going to show an R (Restricted) movie, we had to get written permission from their parents or guardians. We had a form listing all the films that I might show doing the school year, their ratings and why (battle scenes, some swear words etc.) and never had a parent refuse to sign.

Using the headings for Social Studies (World History, U.S. History, Geography, Economic U.S.

Government), English/Literature, Math, Science, Electives, I have listed the material I used, and where possible, how you can track these aids down.

I made an outline requiring my students to either fill in the missing words or supply short answers for each of these films and documentaries, I had an outline requiring my students to either fill in the missing material or short sentence answers. They can all be adapted to an essay assignment.

American History/Social Studies- http://multimedialearning.org/

By far, in my opinion, the best Multimedia presentations on the market. They offered a tremendous amount of professional PowerPoints suitable for use in your classroom. These PowerPoints are available in both PC and Mac presentations. Their catalog includes 33 **U.S. History,** 25 **World History,** and 5 **U.S. Government, and Economics** PowerPoint presentations. You can order individual programs or sets if your school is interested. Over the years, I have purchased all of their PowerPoints and was very impressed, and still am. From these PowerPoint presentations, I created my own note outlines which my students used to "fill-in-the-missing words." This forced them to read along with me, the presented material from each slide, and then find the missing words in their notes. Many of the videos/DVDs can be interchangeable with World

Teaching Material/Exercises/Videos etc.

History, Social Studies, Current Events and even literature. For example, The Crucible can be used as part of U.S. history and Salem Witchcraft Trials or used in English as literature piece.

World History-http://multimedialearning.org/

Multimedia Learning has excellent PowerPoints to use covering World History. I break off from World History when our nation and the world faced WW I. From that point on, I focus on our nation and the events of the world leading to the two world wars together: more of a global view versus focusing solely on U.S. or European countries etc.

Videos/DVD's for Social Studies

Nicholas and Alexandra (DVD) – Shows the events leading to the Russian Revolution, Socialism, and the assassination of the czar, his family, and Rasputin.

A fascinating look at the last, tragic Russian monarchs; the kindly, indecisive Czar Nicholas and his reclusive, fear-haunted Czarina. The story follows their problems from the onset through the introduction of Rasputin to the Russian Court, to the Czar's abdication and the family's execution at Ekaterinburg on July 16, 1918.

Gary J. Rose, Ph.D.

Number of discs: 1 Rated: PG Parental Guidance Suggested Studio: Sony Pictures Home Entertainment
DVD Release Date: July 27, 1999
Run Time: 183 minutes

America: The Story of US – 3-disc collection (Liev Schreiber)

How did the United States become a global superpower? America: The Story of US is an epic 12-hour television event (on DVD) of the event that explores the country's remarkable journey. Broken down in the following DVD's:

1. Rebels
From Jamestown to Plymouth, early settlers fight for survival. Tobacco sows the seeds of opportunity; the north becomes a powerhouse of trade. Tension, taxation, and resistance explode into war as the rebels take on the might of the British Empire.

PG13 Language: English
Runtime: 43 minutes
Release date: April 24, 2010

2. Revolution
The colonies declare independence, taking on the might of the British Empire. Washington's army is near

defeat, but new weapons and battle tactics turn the tide. Forged through revolution, a new nation is born.

TV-PG Subtitles and Closed Captions Language: English
Runtime: 44 minutes
Release date: May 1, 2010

3. Westward/Division
Trailblazing pioneers set out to conquer the west, but find the land already claimed. Wagon trains meet hardship on the road to California's gold. The steamboat ushers in a new era of commerce, industry, and unprecedented wealth.

TV-PG Subtitles and Closed Captions Language: English
Runtime: 44 minutes.
Release date: May 1, 2010

4. Division
Commerce and industry thrive across the new nation, now one of the wealthiest on Earth. The Erie Canal brings big risk and bigger reward. In the South, cotton is king but slavery fuels a growing divide.

TV-PG Subtitles and Closed Captions Language: English
Runtime: 43 minutes
Release date: May 8, 2010

5. Civil War
The Civil War rages. The formidable Confederate army cannot match the Union's mastery of technology; railroads, supply lines, and the telegram become new weapons in a modern war.

TV- PG Subtitles and Closed Captions Language: English
Runtime: 44 minutes
Release date: May 8, 2010

6. Heartland
The Transcontinental Railroad unites the nation and transforms the Heartland. Native American civilizations decline as farmers settle the continent.

TV-PG Subtitles and Closed Captions Language: English
Runtime: 43 minutes
Release date: May 8, 2010

7. Cities/Boom
Americans conquer a new frontier: the modern city, with Carnegie's empire of steel as its backbone. Skyscrapers and the Statue of Liberty are symbols of the American Dream for millions of immigrants.

TV-PGSubtitles and Closed Captions Language: English
Runtime: 44 minutes

Teaching Material/Exercises/Videos etc.

Release date: May 15, 2010

8. Boom
America strikes oil and the boom time begins. Henry Ford brings the motorcar to the masses; the nation hits the road. Massive engineering projects modernize the West.

TV-PG Subtitles and Closed Captions Language: English Runtime: 44 minutes
Release date: May 22, 2010

9. Bust
Boom turns to bust when the stock market crashes. The Great Depression and the dust bowl blanket the nation in darkness. Roosevelt's New Deal signals recovery.

TV-PG Subtitles and Closed Captions Language: English
Runtime: 44 minutes
Release date: May 22, 2010

10. WW II
The attack on Pearl Harbor brings America into World War. The war effort revitalizes the nation's economy. American innovation and manufacturing might invigorate the Allies in Europe and in the Pacific.

TV-PG Subtitles and Closed Captions Language: English
Runtime: 44 minutes
Release date: May 29, 2010

11. Superpower

America becomes a global superpower; the economy and population boom. In the jet age and the space age, pioneers conquer new frontiers and run headlong into Cold War.

TV-PG Subtitles and Closed Captions Language: English
Runtime: 44 minutes
Release date: May 30, 2010

12. Millennium

The Cold War is the first test for the new superpower. The Challenger disaster and 9/11 are tragedies that challenge the nation. From the television to the credit card and the personal computer, technology drives America into the 21st Century.

TV-PG Subtitles and Closed Captions Language: English
Runtime: 44 minutes
Release date: July 3, 2010

Teaching Material/Exercises/Videos etc.

The Men Who Built America – History Channel DVD

John D. Rockefeller, Cornelius Vanderbilt, Andrew Carnegie, Henry Ford, and J.P. Morgan rose from obscurity and in the process built modern America. Their names hang on street signs, are etched into buildings and are a part of the fabric of history. These men created the American Dream and were the engine of capitalism as they transformed everything they touched in building the oil, rail, steel, shipping, automobile and finance industries. Their paths crossed repeatedly as they elected presidents, set economic policies and influenced major events of the 50 most formative years this country has ever known. From the Civil War to the Great Depression and World War I, they led the way.

Number of discs: 3
Rated: NR
DVD Release Date: January 22, 2013
Run Time: 360 minutes

The World Wars – (Don Meehan)

Adolf Hitler. Franklin Delano Roosevelt. Benito Mussolini. Winston Churchill. Charles de Gaulle. George Patton. Before they were the giants of WWII, they were infantrymen and privates in WWI, the "war to end all wars." THE WORLD WARS from

Gary J. Rose, Ph.D.

HISTORY(R) brings you the story of the devastating three decades of 20th-century world war through the eyes of the men whose characters were forged in the trenches before they commanded a world on the brink of disaster. See how, from Ypres and the Somme to the Battle of the Bulge and the invasion of Normandy, the iconic figures of WWII became synonymous with either battlefield glory or murderous fascism.

Number of discs: 1
Studio: A&E Home Video
DVD Release Date: September 9, 2014
Run Time: 270 minutes

The Crossing – Story of the Battle of Trenton

The Crossing is a stirring dramatization of General George Washington's surprise attack on the British Army's German mercenaries and the Battle of Trenton. Based on the book by Howard Fast, The Crossing brings to life Washington's historic passage across the Delaware River on Christmas night, 1776 and the lopsided fight that followed.

Number of discs: 1
Rated: NR
Studio: A&E Home Video
DVD Release Date: January 14, 2003
Run Time: 89 minutes

Teaching Material/Exercises/Videos etc.

Founding Fathers – History Channel DVD

They were the most legendary and respected politicians, statesmen and warriors of history's first republic since the days of ancient Rome. They were also traitors and smugglers, rabble rousers and hot-heads, unfaithful husbands and prodigious drinkers. Because despite what some history books and much folklore would have us believe, our nation's revered "Founding Fathers" were, in fact, human beings. Now, in this comprehensive four-part series, gain a fascinating, engagingly intimate glimpse behind the iconic images on the marble busts and the noble faces gazing out from our dollar bills and pocket change. And discover the remarkable, unseen private sides of the men who risked their reputations, fortunes, and lives for the cause of American independence.

DISC 1: Rebels With A Cause / Taking Liberties
DISC 2: You Say You Want A Revolution? / A Healthy Constitution
Number of discs: 2
Rated: NR Studio: A&E Entertainment
DVD Release Date: January 10, 2012
Run Time: 200 minutes

The Presidents – History Channel DVD

THE PRESIDENTS is an unprecedented eight-part survey of the personal lives and legacies of the

Gary J. Rose, Ph.D.

remarkable men who have presided over the Oval Office. From George Washington to George W. Bush, THE PRESIDENTS gathers together vivid snapshots of all 43 Commanders in Chief who have guided America throughout its history--their powerful personalities, weaknesses, and major achievements or historical insignificance. Based on the book To the Best of My Ability, edited by Pulitzer Prize-winner James McPherson, THE PRESIDENTS features rare and unseen photographs and footage, unexpected insight and trivia from journalists, scholars, and politicians such as Walter Cronkite, David Brinkley, Wesley Clark, Bob Dole, and former President Jimmy Carter. Viewed within the changing contexts of each administration, the Presidency has never seemed more compelling and human. Narrated by Edward Herrmann (The Aviator), this three-DVD set is a proud addition to the award-winning documentary tradition of THE HISTORY CHANNEL®. DVD Features: Feature-length Bonus Program "All The Presidents' Wives"; Timeline of U.S. Presidents; Interactive Menus; Scene Selection

Number of discs: 3
Rated: NR Studio: A&E Home Video
DVD Release Date: May 31, 2005
Run Time: 360 minutes

Teaching Material/Exercises/Videos etc.

The States (How the states took shape)

When the founding fathers drew the first map of America, they confronted many of the same challenges that unite and divide us today. HOW THE STATES GOT THEIR SHAPES explores how our borders evolved--and continue to change--in response to religion, transportation, communication, politics, culture clashes, and even Mother Nature. This is no textbook-style documentary series. Local experts and everyday folks lead host Brian Unger, a journalist and former Daily Show correspondent, to insights about some of America s most baffling questions. How are flying fish threatening to re-draw the shape of Illinois? What does the use of cell phones by Pennsylvania s Amish have to do with the shape of their state? How is the phrase sold down the river linked to the shape of what might be our 51st state? Why did the invention of air conditioning change how America picks its Presidents? Unger uncovers the answers, hidden in our map.

BONUS FEATURES: Feature-length HISTORY Special How The States Got Their Shapes
DISC 1: A River Runs Through It / The Great Plains, Trains, & Automobiles / Force of Nature / State of Rebellion
DISC 2: Living on the Edge / Use it Or Lose It / Church and States / A Boom With A View
DISC 3: Culture Clash / Mouthing Off
DISC 4: Bonus Special: How the States Got Their Shapes

Gary J. Rose, Ph.D.

Number of discs: 4
Rated: NR Studio: A&E Entertainment
DVD Release Date: November 1, 2011
Run Time: 420 minutes

The Bible – Epic Miniseries (used during comparative religions)

From Executive Producers Roma Downey and Mark Burnett comes The Bible — an epic 10-part miniseries retelling stories from the Scriptures for a whole new generation. Breathtaking in scope and scale, The Bible features powerful performances, exotic locales and dazzling visual effects that breathe spectacular life into the dramatic tales of faith and courage from Genesis through Revelation. This historic television event is sure to entertain and inspire the whole family.

This 10-part miniseries meets the overwhelming challenge of bringing the story of the Bible to film in a way that embraces modern technology and makes the stories seem relevant and fresh to today's audiences. *The Bible* was truly a project of passion for executive producers Mark Burnett and Roma Downey. By focusing on hope and love as the string of continuity throughout the Bible from Genesis to Revelation, Burnett, Roma, and the writers and filmmakers have created a powerful series about a historical text that's at once action film, adventure, and even love story. The many stories included in this presentation include those of Adam and Eve, Noah and the ark, the birth of Abraham's son Isaac, Moses's parting of the Red Sea, David and Goliath, Samson and Delilah, Mary's conception of Jesus and his birth, the crucifixion of Jesus, and the spread of Jesus's word through his disciples. Each of the 10 episodes is powerfully rendered--the subject matter is by nature moving, and the costuming, special effects, settings, and filming choices are fitting and realistic. The performances of the entire cast are stirring, but special recognition is deserved by Diogo Morgado for his performance as Jesus, Downey as Mother Mary, Darwin Shaw as Peter, Joe Wredden as Judas, and William Houston as Moses.

Please note: Some scenes that were shown when The Bible aired may not be included in this release. These missing scenes are an artistic choice, not a defect. Note: The Packaging of the title comes in such a way that a single case is designed to hold all the 4 discs for the title.

Number of discs: 4
Rated: PG-13 Parents Strongly Cautioned
Studio: 20th Century Fox
DVD Release Date: April 8, 2014
Run Time: 491 minutes

Lincoln and the Civil War (History Channel DVD)

This collection provides a rich portrait of one of the most beloved U.S. Presidents and significant events that surrounded him. Utilizing interviews with leading Lincoln biographers, *Lincoln* explores the inner conflicts that plagued and inspired the man who called himself «the loneliest man in the world.» In a ploy that was ultimately foiled by the Secret Service, *Stealing Lincoln's Body* documents the outrageous 1876 plot to steal Lincoln›s body and hold it for ransom. *The Hunt for John Wilkes Booth* follows Booth, and his co-conspirator David Herold, as they elude more than 10,000 Federal troops for 12 days after assassinating Lincoln. *Sherman's March* re-creates the 285 mile march from Atlanta to Savannah, Georgia, on which Sherman said the effort needed to «make old and young, rich and poor, feel the hard hand of war.»

HISTORY CLASSICS: LINCOLN AND THE CIVIL WAR contains 4 feature-length documentaries on 4 DVDs.

DISC 1 Lincoln / Bonus
DISC 2 Stealing Lincoln's Body
DISC 3 The Hunt For John Wilkes Booth
DISC 4 Sherman's March / Bonus
Rated: NR
Studio: A&E HOME VIDEO
DVD Release Date: September 18, 2012
Run Time: 400 minutes

The Crucible (Play based on Salem Witchcraft Trials – used before Halloween)

DVD Produced in 1996. Stars Daniel Day Lewis and Winona Rider.

Teaching Material/Exercises/Videos etc.

This is a wonderful film that makes various artistic choices to transfer the characters and plot from a play to a film. If you are viewing this as a way of aiding comprehension of the play, be aware that the film-makers break up certain scenes, re-ordering the events, relocate many scenes to take place outdoors and to include more physical movement and action, add and subtract dialogue to editorialize somewhat and to steer the viewer towards a certain, typical interpretation of the play. Also, the film-makers opted to include the normally omitted 2nd scene of Act II of the play, to invent a visit of Abigail to Proctor's jail-cell in which she tries to convince him to run away with her, and to add a scene at the end where we see Proctor hung with two other accused witches (reminiscent of you know who). These changes do make the play more filmic and, perhaps, interesting for a modern audience, but I find the last two issues unfortunate holywoodizations. Strong performances all around.

Running time 124 minutes, Rated PG13 One Disk

Christmas Unwrapped – The History of Christmas (History Channel DVD)

Every December 25 Christians throughout the world join together in celebration of Christ's birth. But where do these various Christmas traditions come from? Why for instance is the holiday marked by the giving and receiving of gifts? And who came up with the idea of a Christmas tree? In this special presentation from THE HISTORY CHANNEL-? take an enchanting journey through the past of one of the world's most recognized holidays. Trace the emergence of the modern-day Christmas celebration from pagan festivals such as the Roman Saturnalia and learn how British settlers in the New World transformed the patron saint of children into the enduring figure of Santa Claus. These fascinating mysteries-and many more-are revealed in CHRISTMAS UNWRAPPED: THE HISTORY OF CHRISTMAS.

The Haunted History of Halloween (History Channel DVD)

Like Christmas Unwrapped, this A&E special, which pops up every year around Halloween, is hosted by Harry Smith. It tells the history of Christmas dating from the time of the Druidic festival of Samhain right up to the 20th century. Along the way noted scholars and authors are interviewed as the roots of Halloween are traced over the centuries. Clips from horror films such as Halloween are included. Also discussed is Mexico's Day of the Dead holiday and various cities are visited to explore their Halloween traditions and festivities. It's a bit of a fluffy pieces but it's all good fun and I still enjoy watching it each Halloween season.

Teaching Material/Exercises/Videos etc.

History of Thanksgiving (History Channel DVD)

Thanksgiving is one of my favorite times of the year, coming as it does between Halloween and Christmas. I realized long ago that the true story of Thanksgiving is somewhat different from the one I learned growing up in a small Midwestern farming community in the 50's and 60's. This TV show may have clarified some of those misconceptions, but it certainly did nothing to diminish my enjoyment of the holiday. In the end, does it really matter if venison and lobster were served instead of pumpkin pie and turkey or if the Native Americans weren't invited so much as just showed up to see what all the noise was about?

Number of discs: 1
Rated: NR
Studio: A&E Home Video
Release Date: November 11, 2010

The Nazis – A Warning From History (History Channel/BBC production) 2015

How could a political party as fundamentally evil and overtly racist as the Nazis come to power? This remains one of the most enigmatic questions of the last century. Acclaimed historian Laurence Rees examines what led a cultured nation at the heart of Europe to commit the atrocities it did. In so doing, he exposes popular myths and encourages understanding of the real forces that led to one of the darkest chapters in modern history. Was it simply the hypnotic power of Hitler's rhetoric? Did the Gestapo really impose themselves by terror on an unwilling population? Through interviews with witnesses and perpetrators, along with archive film and records, this six-part series unveils a more chilling reality.

Number of discs: 2
Rated: NR
Studio: BBC
DVD Release Date: August 25, 2015
Run Time: 300 minutes

The Bunker (Hitler's last days)

Anthony Hopkins gives an Emmy Award-winning performance as Adolf Hitler over the 105 days of his decline. With the Third Reich crumbling around him, Hitler rages as he faces the final hours before a choice must be made between suicide and surrender.

Number of discs: 1
Rated: R Restricted
Studio: HBO
DVD Release Date: April 30, 2013
Run Time: 150 minutes

Teaching Material/Exercises/Videos etc.

Modern Marvels – The Manhattan Project (History Channel)

At 5:30 a.m., July 16, 1945, scientists and dignitaries awaited the detonation of the first atomic bomb in a desolate area of the New Mexico desert aptly known as Jornada del Muerto--Journey of Death. Dubbed the Manhattan Project, the top-secret undertaking was tackled with unprecedented speed and expense--almost $30-billion in today's dollars. Los Alamos scientists and engineers relate their trials, triumphs, and dark doubts about building the ultimate weapon of war in the interest of peace.

Number of discs: 1
Rated: NR
Studio: A&E Home Video
DVD Release Date: August 30, 2005
Run Time: 50 minutes

Japanese War Crimes (DVD)

Over 14 dreadful years between 1932 and 1945 Japan went on a rampage of war and atrocity beyond comprehension. American survivors of the Bataan Death March, torpedoed hellships and slave mines tell hair-raising stories, firmly illustrated by never-before-seen film footage and stark illustrations.

Number of discs: 1

Gary J. Rose, Ph.D.

Rated: NR
Studio: A&E Home Video
DVD Release Date: September 1, 2004

Pearl Harbor (The Movie)

History comes alive in the unforgettable epic motion picture PEARL HARBOR, the spectacular blockbuster brought to the screen by Jerry Bruckheimer and Michael Bay. Astounding visual and audio effects put you at the center of the event that changed the world -- that early Sunday morning in paradise when warplanes screamed across the peaceful skies of Pearl Harbor and jolted America into World War II. This real-life tale of catastrophic defeat, heroic victory, and personal courage focuses on the war's devastating impact on two daring young pilots, Ben Affleck (ARMAGEDDON) and Josh Hartnet (THE VIRGIN SUICIDES), and a beautiful, dedicated nurse, Kate Beckinsale (SERENDIPITY). PEARL HARBOR is extraordinary moviemaking -- a breathtaking reenactment of the "date which will live in infamy" and a heartfelt tribute to the men and women who lived it.

Number of discs: 1
Rated: PG-13 Parents Strongly Cautioned
Studio: TOUCHSTONE PICTURES
DVD Release Date: December 4, 2001
Run Time: 183 minutes

Teaching Material/Exercises/Videos etc.

(NOTE): I did not show this film until after I lectured my students about the cause of the attack, the planning of the attack (fins put on Japanese torpedoes) and mistakes made by our military. While watching the film, I point out those areas. I did the same with the next listed movie, Titanic

Titanic - DVD

Nothing on Earth can rival the epic spectacle and breathtaking grandeur of *Titanic,* the sweeping love story that sailed into the hearts of moviegoers around the world, ultimately emerging as the most popular motion picture of all time. Leonardo DiCaprio and Oscar-nominee Kate Winslet light up the screen as Jack and Rose, the young lovers who find one another on the maiden voyage of the "unsinkable" R.M.S. Titanic. But when the doomed luxury liner collides with an iceberg in the frigid North Atlantic their passionate love affair becomes a thrilling race for survival. From acclaimed filmmaker James Cameron comes a tale of forbidden love and courage in the face of disaster that triumphs as a true cinematic masterpiece.

Number of discs: 1
Rated: PG-13 Parents Strongly Cautioned
Studio: Paramount
DVD Release Date: August 31, 1999
Run Time: 194 minutes

Gary J. Rose, Ph.D.

The Green Beret DVD

An editorial by Jeff Shannon did a good job discussing this film. On Amazon, he states, "Anyone who fought in Vietnam can tell you that the war bore little resemblance to this propagandistic action film starring and co-directed by John Wayne. But the film itself is not nearly as bad as its reputation would suggest; critics roasted its gung-ho politics while ignoring its merits as an exciting (if rather conventional and idealistic) war movie. Some notorious mistakes were made--in the final shot, the sun sets in the east!--and it's an awkward attempt to graft WWII heroics onto the Vietnam experience. But as the Duke's attempt to acknowledge the men who were fighting and dying overseas, it's a rousing film in which Wayne commands a regiment on a mission to kidnap a Viet Cong general. David Janssen plays a journalist who learns to understand Wayne's commitment to battling Communism, and Jim Hutton (Timothy's dad) plays an ill-fated soldier who adopts a Vietnamese orphan.

I showed this film to give my students an idea of what it was like out in the jungle, the V.C., the tunnels etc. This parlayed into the DVD – *Tunnel Rats*.

Number of discs: 1
Rated: G General Audience
Studio: Warner Home Video
DVD Release Date: October 29, 1997
Run Time: 142 minutes

Teaching Material/Exercises/Videos etc.

Suicide Missions Tunnel Rats History Channel Vietnam War

This is a great DVD by the History Channel of the men who served in the Vietnam War as "Tunnel Rats." These were extremely brave men – lightly armed, that went directly into the underground tunnels of the Viet Cong to do battle one on one with the enemy.

Disk: 1
Running time 50 minutes
History Channel.

Bataan Death March DVD

An oral history of the shocking abuse inflicted on U.S. and Filipino P.O.W.s as their Japanese captors marched them day and night, without food or medicine, for over 50 miles. Many died enroute to the camp, but many more were shot, bayoneted, or beheaded by prison guards. We follow one survivor as he returns to Bataan for the first time.

Number of discs: 1
Studio: A&E Television Networks
DVD Release Date: July 17, 2008
Run Time: 50 minutes

Gary J. Rose, Ph.D.

Tuskegee Airmen DVD

This is the original film prior to the remake, Red Tails. Featuring an all-star cast headed by Laurence Fishburne, fireballs of high speed air action explode off the screen in this exciting story of the "Fighting 99th," the first squadron of black American pilots to be allowed to fight for their country. Based on the true story.

Number of discs: 1
Rated: PG-13 Parental Guidance Suggested
Studio: HBO Home Video
DVD Release Date: January 23, 2001
Run Time: 106 minutes

Red Tails DVD

1944. As the war in Europe continues to take its toll on Allied forces; the Pentagon brass has no recourse but to consider unorthodox options -- including the untried and untested African-American pilots of the experimental Tuskegee training program. Just as the young Tuskegee men are on the brink of being shut down and shipped back home; they are given the ultimate chance to show their courage. Against all the odds; with something to prove and everything to lose; these intrepid young airmen take to the skies to fight for their country -- and the fate of the free world.

Teaching Material/Exercises/Videos etc.

Number of discs: 1
Rated: PG-13 Parents Strongly Cautioned
Studio: 20th Century Fox
DVD Release Date: May 22, 2012
Run Time: 125 minutes

Note: I used both of these films (alternating which one to use) for discussions on racism and discrimination.

Memphis Bell DVD

Jeff Shannon editorial for Amazon on this film states: If you've never seen an aviation movie before in your entire life, you'll be blissfully ignorant of the fact that *Memphis Belle* shamelessly (and yet gloriously) incorporates just about every cliché in the flight-movie handbook. If you're a big fan of aviation movies--especially movies about World War II bomber crews--you'll be glad that the genre's clichés have been handled with such professional flair. As it follows the crew of a B-17 bomber on its final and most dangerous mission over Germany, *Memphis Belle* may be little more than a slick and highly authentic presentation of familiar thrills and characters, but it's a rousing piece of entertainment. Featuring an ensemble cast of fresh faces who've since enjoyed thriving careers (including Billy Zane, Sean Astin, Eric Stoltz, D.B. Sweeney, and Harry Connick Jr.), the movie exists as a fitting tribute to the men who fought and often died in the air over hostile territory. It's the Hollywood version of a 1944 wartime documentary made by legendary director William Wyler (whose daughter served as one of this film's producers), and as such it's a bit contrived and melodramatic. And yet, this exciting movie is almost certain to grab and hold your attention, offering an honorable reminder of the bravery and integrity that were crucial ingredients of any bomber's crew.

Number of discs: 1
Rated: PG-13 Parents Strongly Cautioned
Studio: Warner Bros. Pictures
DVD Release Date: May 27, 1998
Run Time: 107 minutes

Memorial Day DVD

When SSgt. Kyle Vogel leaves a handwritten letter on the seat of his car, grabs a pistol and steps into a Minnesota forest, we wonder who he is and what he's about to do. Flash back a few months as Vogel lies wounded in a hospital near Anbar Province, Iraq. The night before he's due to return to combat, his doctor, Lt. Kelly Tripp, presses him on why he's so obsessed with collecting battle souvenirs. Kyle proceeds to tell her what happened on Memorial Day, 1993, when, as a 13-year old boy, he discovered his Grandpa Bud's WWII footlocker. Though reluctant to talk about the war, Bud, who served with the 82nd Airborne, strikes a deal with Kyle: "Pick any three objects, and I'll tell you the story behind each one." As we see Bud's WWII tales from Europe, we also see how Kyle's experiences in Iraq have paralleled them—and how that day on the porch will affect how he ultimately deals with the losses, regrets and moral dilemmas that unite all soldiers across wars and generations.

Number of discs: 1
Rated: NR
Studio: Image Entertainment
DVD Release Date: May 29, 2012
Run Time: 104 minutes

Forrest Gump DVD

Hanks is Forrest Gump, who despite being mentally challenged, tried hard, is honest and places his trust in luck. He tells his life story to anyone who sits next to him at a bus stop, and the flashbacks follow Forrest and his good heart through some of the highlights of modern American history. Through the use of digital imagery, Forrest appears to interact in scenes with John F. Kennedy, John Lennon and George Wallace. "Life is like a box of chocolates."

Note: Excellent Social Studies piece. Great film to display after you cover U.S. History to the 1970s.

Number of discs: 2
Rated: PG-13 Parents Strongly Cautioned
Studio: Paramount

Gary J. Rose, Ph.D.

DVD Release Date: August 28, 2001
Run Time: 141 minutes

Saving Private Ryan DVD

Tom Hanks, Matt Damon, Edward Burns. An explosive WWII drama in which Private James Ryan becomes the object of a desperate and dangerous rescue mission in war-torn Germany after authorities learn his three other brothers already have been killed in combat.

Number of discs: 1
Rated: R Restricted
Studio: Dreamworks Video
DVD Release Date: May 25, 2004
Run Time: 169 minutes

Note: I generally show this film to emphasize how bloody the Normandy landings were.

U.S.S. Indianapolis-Mission of the Shark DVD

True story of the sinking of the U.S.S. Indianapolis after delivering the first atomic bomb and the struggles the sailors endured for days in shark-infested waters until rescue. It further covers the captain's scape-goat court-martial.

Number of discs: 1
Rated: NR

Teaching Material/Exercises/Videos etc.

Studio: MGM (Video & DVD)
DVD Release Date: July 31, 2007
Run Time: 100 minutes

Race (DVD)

Based on the incredible true story of Jesse Owens, the legendary athletic superstar whose quest to become the greatest track and field athlete in history thrusts him onto the world stage of the 1936 Olympics, where he faces off against Adolf Hitler's vision of Aryan supremacy. "Race" is an enthralling film about courage, determination, tolerance, and friendship, and an inspiring drama about one man's fight to become an Olympic legend.

Number of discs: 1
Rated: PG-13 Parents Strongly Cautioned
Studio: Universal Pictures Home Entertainment
DVD Release Date: May 31, 2016
Run Time: 135 minutes

The Hindenberg Disaster (DVD)

George C. Scott leads an all-star cast in The Hindenburg, a gripping suspense thriller that attempts to reveal the intricate plots behind the historic airship disaster of 1937. Assigned as a colonel by the German government to prevent any plans of sabotage during the Hindenburg's transatlantic voyage, Franz Ritter

(Scott) suspects everyone aboard the luxury ship, especially a German countess (Bancroft) vehemently opposed to the Nazi regime. Stylishly directed by Robert Wise and co-starring Burgess Meredith, Gig Young, Charles Durning and Richard Dysart, The Hindenburg brings to life one of aviation's most infamous events in history and one of the screen's most engrossing mysteries.

This film is a compendium of the facts and fiction of the events leading to the disaster. For dramatic effect, sabotage was chosen as the cause, rather than electricity lashing out at a couple of tons of hydrogen.

Number of discs: 1
Rated: PG Parental Guidance Suggested
Studio: Universal Pictures Home Entertainment
Release Date: December 25, 1975
Run Time: 127 minutes

The 20th Century DVD series

Witness the most significant events from the last 100 years in this dynamic new 6 DVD collection! This salute to the Twentieth Century showcases the global milestones, remarkable achievements and legendary figures that shook and shaped the world in which we live. Through insightful narration, rare photographs and stunning footage, this fascinating collection ventures through the pop-culture and historical highlights that paved the way for future generations.

Teaching Material/Exercises/Videos etc.

From politics to Pac-Man, prepare to travel through the decades of the Twentieth Century!

CONTENTS:

Disc 1 1900s and 1910s

Witness the birth of an era that changed the world forever. From the first flight of the Wright Brothers to the sinking of the Titanic, these were the decades of great change and coming of age for many modern societies. With the beginning and end of WWI still lingering and a sense of unrest and reform for much of the world, many seized the opportunity and sparked revolution and rebellion into all aspects of their lives.

Disc 2 1920s and 1930s

The Roaring '20s rang in hot with the prohibition of alcohol in the U.S. This piece of legislation marked a social and cultural trend that redefined modern society. Sadly, the decade ended with the deviating crash of the stock market and the day know as Black Friday. Amidst the drought and depression in America rose a new leader in Germany, Hitler. From the Nazi invasions in Europe to the catastrophes of The Spanish Civil War, explore the decades of creation and destruction that brought the world to their senses.

Gary J. Rose, Ph.D.

Disc 3 1940s and 1950s

The devastating events of WWII had profound effects worldwide. The consequences of the deadliest conflict in human history lingered for decades to come. However, with the rise and fall of the Nazi Regime came a booming economy that influenced and improved the post-war era. From the baby boom to the legendary beginnings of Marilyn Monroe and Elvis, the decades of the 40s and 50s introduced a distinctly different society and culture of change and progress.

Disc 4 1960s and 1970s

Revolution, rebellion and rock and roll brought a series of firsts for the decades of the 60s and 70s. From the first man on the moon and the raging objection over the War in Vietnam to the Assassination of JFK and the Watergate Scandal, the complex decay of social order liberated a generation unrecognizable to the previous. Filled with new thoughts about cultural, social and political norms, these were the years that broke free from the constraints of previous generations to create some of the most significant advancements of the 20th Century.

Disc 5 1980s and 1990s

With the dawning of a new millennium in the near future and the remarkable technical and social

Teaching Material/Exercises/Videos etc.

advances created during this time, the final decades of the 20th Century are incomparable to any other. From the global tragedies of the Challenger Explosion and the nuclear disaster in Chernobyl to the remarkable advancements in global communication via the internet, these are the remarkable events that defined an era and brought a sense of economic liberation and multiculturalism never felt before.

Disc 6 BONUS DISC The Decade You Were Born 1940s-1980s

Number of discs: 6
Rated: NR Studio: Mill Creek Entertainment
DVD Release Date: May 20, 2014
Run Time: 1280 minutes

9-11 DVD

Originally broadcast on CBS in March 2002, *9/11* is an extraordinary record of that fateful day in New York City. This one-of-a-kind documentary was originally conceived as a portrait of 21-year-old Tony Benetatos, a firefighter trainee at Manhattan›s Duane Street firehouse, located seven blocks from the World Trade Center. By the time filming was finished, brothers Jules and Gedeon Naudet had captured history in the making, including the only image of the first jetliner striking Tower 1, and the only footage from *within* the tower as it collapsed. This is not, however, a film

Gary J. Rose, Ph.D.

about the murderous nightmare of terrorism. It's the ultimate rite-of-passage drama, more immediate and meaningful than any fiction film could be, with Benetatos and his supportive colleagues emerging as heroes of the first order. Sensitively narrated by codirector and fellow firefighter James Hanlon, *9/11* will endure forever as a tribute to those, living and dead, who witnessed hell on that sunny Tuesday morning. --*Jeff Shannon Amazon*

Number of discs: 1
Rated: NR Studio: Paramount
DVD Release Date: September 12, 2002
Run Time: 112 minutes

Why the Towers Fell - An Exclusive Investigation into the Collapse of the World Trade Center

For most people the image of the collapse of the World Trade Center Towers on September 11, 2001, was not only a scene of unforgettable horror, it was a moment of unimaginable consequence. Within days, NOVA began following a blue-ribbon team of forensic engineers as they began searching for clues that would tell them why the towers fell. This moving and informative documentary features interviews with survivors and rescue personnel who recount the buildings' last moments and their harrowing journeys to safety, interweaving these stories with the insights of some of the leading structural engineers in the world to explain exactly what happened on that fateful day. Why the Towers Fell takes viewers through the process by which the investigative team came to understand the how's and why's of one of America's greatest tragedies. From a detailed examination of the building's original design to the relentless process of combing scrap steel yards and Ground Zero itself for evidence, this was one of the most extensive and difficult disaster investigations ever undertaken. The team tested building materials, calculated the role of the jet fuel in the fire, estimated the speed of the aircraft and the damage to the building's core, and they analyzed the effectiveness of the escape and fire protection systems. The conclusions they reached will certainly influence the building of future skyscrapers for years to come.

Number of discs: 1
Rated: NR
Studio: NOVA / PBS
DVD Release Date: June 18, 2002
Run Time: 56 minutes

Flight 93 – The Flight that Fought Back DVD

A defining day in our history. It's an event that shook the world. Honest, unflinching and profoundly moving, United 93 tells the unforgettable story of the heroic passengers and crew members who prevented the terrorists from carrying out their plans for the fourth hijacked plane on September 11, 2001. As on-ground military and civilian teams scrambled to make sense of the unfolding events, forty people sat down as strangers found the courage to stand up as one.

Number of discs:1
Rated: R Restricted
Studio: Universal Pictures Home Entertainment
DVD Release Date: September 6, 2011
Run Time: 111 minutes

Son of the Morning Star DVD

Story of Gen. Custer, Crazy Horse, and Sitting Bull prior, during and after the Battle of Little Big Horn.

Rated: PG-13 Parents Strongly Cautioned
Number of tapes: 1
Run Time: 183 minutes

The Alamo DVD

Acclaimed action epic about one of the most important events in American history! It's the heroic tale of the 200 brave men who made the ultimate sacrifice in the name of freedom defending a small Texas fort for 13 days against an entire army! Commanded by three men -- Lt. Col. William Travis (Patrick Wilson), James Bowie (Patric), and David Crockett (Thornton) -- their against-all-odds courage at the Alamo would forever live on as a rallying cry for liberty and independence!

Teaching Material/Exercises/Videos etc.

Number of discs: 1
Rated: PG-13 Parents Strongly Cautioned
Studio: Buena Vista Home Entertainment
DVD Release Date: September 28, 2004
Run Time: 137 minutes

Last Ounce of Courage DVD

Bob Revere, a small-town war hero, is heartbroken when his own son Tom loses his life defending America. Tom left behind a son of his own named Christian, and 14 years later, the young boy and his mother move back to the small town to be with their family for the holidays. Christian disconnects with his grandfather Bob, as they both are going through the pain of losing a dad and losing a son. When Christian is threatened with school suspension for bringing his bible to school, Bob notices that his country is headed in a dangerous direction and that freedom itself is on the line. Encouraged by his grandson Christian, who asks what did his father die for?, Bob finally takes a stand for his beliefs and finds himself jailed for putting up the towns Christmas tree and refusing to take it down. In this beautiful story of love and forgiveness, they discover a way to unite and to make a difference in their community by claiming their freedom and standing up for their rights.

Number of discs: 1
Rated: PG Parental Guidance Suggested

Studio: MoMo Bay – Gaiam
DVD Release Date: December 4, 2012
Run Time: 101 minutes

Note: Great social studies video.

Patriots Day DVD

Mark Wahlberg shines in this all-star action-thriller that chronicles the courage and power of the people of Boston during the real-life manhunt for the Boston Marathon bombers.

Number of discs: 2
Rated: R Restricted Studio: Lionsgate
DVD Release Date: March 28, 2017
Run Time: 133 minutes

Gran Torino DVD

A disgruntled Korean War vet, Walt Kowalski (Eastwood), sets out to reform his neighbor, a young Hmong teenager, who tried to steal Kowalski's prized possession: his 1972 Gran Torino. It raises a number of issues, including ethnic relations, immigration, economic changes in America, life in urban America, individual violence and conflict resolution. Great for essay writing and debates.

Number of discs: 1

Teaching Material/Exercises/Videos etc.

Rated: R Restricted
Studio: Warner Brothers
DVD Release Date: October 6, 2015

Science

DK Eyewitness Videos

Years ago, Barnes and Noble gave away VHS tapes from DK Videos Productions when you purchased any of their DK books. I was fortunate that on the day of my purchase, the cashier gave me a complete set of their science videos which I show my students, including my incarcerated adults, using a television set equipped with a VHS player. These are great short (25 minutes) videos narrated by Martin Sheen covering all the subjects below. They are great supplemental pieces for your lessons on both General Science and Life Science.

Birds, Butterflies and moths, Artic and Antarctica, Amphibians, Reptiles, Dinosaurs, Human Machine, The Skelton, Fish, Seashore, Ocean, Sharks, Rocks and Minerals, Desert Ponds and Streams, Horse, Insects, Jungle, Apes ,Mammals, Natural Disasters, Weather. Planets. Volcanoes. Plants, Trees, Tide pools, and Survival. These videos are normally listed on eBay.

Gary J. Rose, Ph.D.

Literature

Treasure Island DVD (2012)

Young Jim Hawkins is the only one who can successfully get a schooner to a legendary Island known for buried treasure. But aboard the ship is a mysterious cook named John Silver (Emmy winner Eddie Izzard, The Riches), whose true motivation on the journey challenges Jim s trust in the entire crew. This is an exciting and atmospheric new take on the definitive pirate action adventure of reckless buccaneers, buried fortunes and a friendship forged in peril on the high seas.

Number of discs: 1
Rated: Unrated
Studio: Vivendi Entertainment
DVD Release Date: July 24, 2012
Run Time: 183 minutes

Last of the Mohicans

Great background while teaching the French and Indian War. An epic adventure and passionate romance unfold against the panorama of a frontier wilderness ravaged by war. Academy Award® winner Daniel Day-Lewis (Best Actor in 1989 for My Left Foot) stars as Hawkeye, rugged frontiersman and adopted son of the Mohicans, and Madeleine Stowe is Cora Munro, aristocratic daughter of a proud British Colonel. Their love, tested by fate, blazes amidst a brutal conflict between the British, the French and Native American allies that engulfs the majestic mountains and cathedral-like forests of Colonial America.

Number of discs: 1
Rated: R Restricted
Studio: 20th Century Fox
DVD Release Date: January 23, 2001
Run Time: 117 minutes

The Patriot

Revolutionary War film starring Mel Gibson as Benjamin Martin, a courageous and heroic South Carolina farmer who reluctantly joins the Revolutionary War to avenge a British colonel's brutal and senseless act against his family. Facing off in a climactic battle against the Green Dragoons, the most deadly branch of the British fighting forces led by General Cornwallis (Tom Wilkinson) and Colonel Abington (Jason Isaacs), the peace-loving American must draw on his patriotic fervor and the skills of his son and fellow soldier, Gabriel (Heath Ledger), to help bring about the birth of a nation.

Number of discs: 1
Rated: R Restricted
Studio: Sony

Run Time: 165.00 minutes

Glory

The heart-stopping story of the first black regiment to fight for the North in the Civil War, GLORY stars Matthew Broderick, Denzel Washington, Cary Elwes and Morgan Freeman. Broderick and Elwes are the idealistic young Bostonians who lead the regiment; Freeman is the inspirational sergeant who unites the troops; and Denzel Washington, in an Oscar(r) - winning performance (1989, Best Supporting Actor), is the runaway slave who embodies the indomitable spirit of the 54th Regiment of Massachusetts.

Number of discs: 1
Rated: R Restricted
Studio: Sony Pictures Home Entertainment
DVD Release Date: June 2, 2009
Run Time: 122 minutes

Lincoln

Steven Spielberg directs two-time Academy Award(R) winner Daniel Day-Lewis (Best Actor, THERE WILL BE BLOOD, 2007, and MY LEFT FOOT, 1989) in LINCOLN -- with an all-star ensemble cast including Sally Field, Tommy Lee Jones and Joseph Gordon-Levitt. This inspiring and revealing drama focuses on the 16th President's tumultuous final four months in office as this visionary leader pursues a course of action to end the Civil War, unite the country and abolish slavery. Complete with never-before-seen footage featuring Steven Spielberg and the cast, who take you deep inside the making of the movie, LINCOLN sheds light on a man of moral courage and fierce determination.

Number of discs: 1
Rated: PG-13 Parents Strongly Cautioned
Studio: Walt Disney Studios Home Entertainment
DVD Release Date: March 26, 2013
Run Time: 150 minutes

The Count of Monte Cristo (2002)

Jim Caviezel (HIGH CRIMES) and Guy Pearce (THE TIME MACHINE) give sizzling performances in THE COUNT OF MONTE CRISTO -- the greatest tale of betrayal, adventure, and revenge the world has ever known. When the dashing and guileless Edmond Dantes (Caviezel) is betrayed by his best friend (Pearce) and wrongly imprisoned, he becomes consumed by thoughts of vengeance. After a miraculous escape, he transforms himself into the mysterious and wealthy Count of Monte Cristo, insinuates himself into the French nobility, and puts his cunning plan of revenge in action. This swashbuckling thriller will have you sitting on the edge of your seat until the last ounce of revenge is exacted.

Number of discs: 1
Rated: PG-13 Parents Strongly Cautioned
Studio: Buena Vista Home Video
DVD Release Date: September 10, 2002
Run Time: 131 minutes

Schindler's List

Experience one of the most historically significant films of all time like never before with Steven Spielberg's cinematic masterpiece, Schindler's List. Winner of seven Academy Awards including Best Picture and Best Director, this incredible true story follows the enigmatic Oskar Schindler (Liam Neeson), who saved the lives of more than 1,100 Jews during the Holocaust. It is the triumph of one man who made a difference and the drama of those who survived one of the darkest chapters in human history because of what he did. Meticulously restored from the original film negative in pristine high definition and supervised by Steven Spielberg, Schindler's List is a powerful story whose lessons of courage and faith continue to inspire generations.

Number of discs: 3
Rated: R Restricted
Studio: Universal Pictures Home Entertainment
DVD Release Date: March 5, 2013

Teaching Material/Exercises/Videos etc.

Escape from Sorbibor (Newer release due in 2018)

Based on a true story of one of the most brutal Nazi death camps in eastern Poland, and how the Jews devised, with the help of Russian POW soldiers, an escape.

Number of discs: 1
Rated: NR Not Rated
Studio: Echo Bridge Home Entertainment
DVD Release Date: January 6, 1999
Run Time: 119 minutes

Boy in the Striped Pajamas

Pete Hammond of Hollywood.com describes this film as "Based on the best-selling novel by John Boyne, The Boy in the Striped Pajamas is the tale of curious 8 year-old Bruno. Bored in his new home, Bruno wanders off into the nearby woods where he discovers an unusual fence, behind which is a boy strangely dressed in "black- and-white pajamas." Bruno embarks in a most unusual friendship with the boy, one that proves both ordinary and remarkable, both inspiring and tragic in this "unforgettable motion picture experience."

Number of discs: 1
Rated: PG-13 Parents Strongly Cautioned
Studio: Miramax Lionsgate
DVD Release Date: April 26, 2011
Run Time: 94 minutes

Gary J. Rose, Ph.D.

Silent Night

Great social studies film to show before Christmas break – good discussion piece.

Linda Hamilton, Cassian Bopp, Michael Elkin. On Christmas Eve 1944, three American soldiers and three German soldiers confront the realities of war and discover the true meaning of courage, as well as the true spirit of a blessed night. Based on real events.

Number of discs: 1
Rated: NR
Studio: Platinum Disc/ Mill Creek Entertainment
DVD Release Date: November 8, 2005
Run Time: 86 minutes

Devil's Arithmetic

Based on the popular novel by Jane Yolen, a typical American teenager gets transported back in time and experiences firsthand the horrors of the Holocaust and discovers the meaning of her family's heritage.

Number of discs: 1
Rated: NR
Studio: Showtime Ent.
DVD Release Date: September 21, 2004
Run Time: 95 minutes

Teaching Material/Exercises/Videos etc.

National Geographic - Lewis & Clark - Great Journey West

Relive one of the greatest tales of adventure and exploration in history as National Geographic brings to life the epic journey of Lewis and Clark and their guide Sacagawea and their brave trip to discovery of the land that would become the United States.

Number of discs: 1
Rated: G General Audience
Studio: National Geographic Video
DVD Release Date: May 6, 2003
Run Time: 60 minutes

The Donner Party - movie (2010)

Based on the harrowing true story, THE DONNER PARTY picks up after William Hastings steers a group, nicknamed "Forlorn Hope," off course by promising a shorter route to California through the Sierra Nevada Mountains. After several early snowstorms, the group and its leaders, William Foster (Crispin Glover, Alive in Wonderland, Beowulf) and William Eddy (Clayne Crawford, "24," "CSI"), find themselves lost, freezing and without any source of food. The threat of death and imminent starvation dissolves the group's camaraderie as they are forced to sacrifice one another as a source of nourishment. Surviving only on the flesh of the fallen members of their party, the remaining travelers must weigh their consciences against their will to survive.

Number of discs: 1
Rated: R Restricted
Studio: Alchemy / Millennium
DVD Release Date: January 26, 2010
Run Time: 95 minutes

Pompeii - The Last Day/Colosseum - A Gladiator's Story - Verus and Priscus date from the inaugural games of the Colosseum, at that time known as the Flavian Amphitheatre, built by Emperor Vespasian and opened by his son, Titus. Verus and Priscus were both slaves, caught in different parts of the empire during different wars, but ended up in the same quarry and had the same fate, to be selected and trained as gladiators for Rome.

The documentary works to dispel many of the false notions about gladiators and similar entertainments of the time. Many gladiators were not slaves, but rather willing participants after fame and fortune. Most gladiators did not die in the arena - in fact, survival chances were as high as ninety percent, and those who were injured got the best medical care in Rome. While animals were used as entertainment, often they would cower at the sound of the crowd and the overwhelming sense of being surrounded, which surely must have affected the human participants, too.

Teaching Material/Exercises/Videos etc.

20,000 Leagues Beneath the Sea - Professor Arronax and Ned Land meet Captain Nemo, who reveals that the so-called sea monster they've been told about is actually his submarine The Nautilus.

The Conspirator (2012) - Mary Surratt is the lone female charged as a co-conspirator in the assassination trial of Abraham Lincoln. As the whole nation turns against her, she is forced to rely on her reluctant lawyer to uncover the truth and save her life.

The Presidents - THE PRESIDENTS is an unprecedented eight-part survey of the personal lives and legacies of the remarkable men who have presided over the Oval Office. This highly acclaimed collection now includes a special BIOGRAPHY of President Barack Obama.

From 1789 to today, THE PRESIDENTS collection gathers together vivid snapshots of all Commanders in Chief who have guided America throughout its history - their powerful personalities, weaknesses, and major achievements or historical insignificance. Based on the book *To the Best of My Ability*, edited by Pulitzer Prize-winner James McPherson, THE PRESIDENTS features rare and unseen photographs and footage, unexpected insight and trivia from journalists, scholars, and politicians such as Walter Cronkite, David Brinkley, Wesley Clark, Bob Dole, and former President Jimmy Carter. Viewed within the changing contexts of each administration, the Presidency has never seemed more compelling and human.

Narrated by Edward Herrmann, this four-DVD set is a proud addition to the award-winning documentary tradition of HISTORY.

The Babe - John Goodman (O Brother, Where Art Thou?) brings the legendary Babe Ruth to life in this triumphant film Entertainment Weekly calls "a crowd pleaser."Co-starring Kelly McGillis (Witness), The Babe chronicles Ruth's phenomenal story - from his hard knock beginnings at Baltimore orphanage, to his meteoric rise to baseball superstardom and his poignant retirement from the game. His amazing life and career included seven American League pennants, four World Series championships, two tempestuous marriages and a wild lifestyle that earned him numerous suspensions. The Babe is the definitive story of one of sport's most fascinating figures, capturing all the drama and excitement of the greatest player in baseball history.

Miracle - Filled with exhilarating nonstop hockey action and heart-racing suspense, it's the inspiring true story behind one of the greatest moments in sports history â" the 1980 United States ice hockey team's triumphant Olympic victory against the Soviet Union. Kurt Russell gives a brilliant performance as the dynamic and determined coach Herb Brooks, who had an impossible dream -- beat the seemingly unbeatable

Soviets at their own game. Starting with a handpicked group of twenty-six undisciplined kids, Brooks coached them to play like they never played before, and turned twenty of them into a team that believed they could achieve the unachievable -- and in the process, united a nation with a new feeling of hope.

Seabiscuit - A great American story from Academy Award-nominated filmmaker Gary Ross, Seabiscuit stars Tobey Maguire, Jeff Bridges and Chris Cooper. Based on the inspiring true story of three men - a jockey, a trainer and a businessman - and the undersized racehorse who took the entire nation on the ride of a lifetime.

The Unlocking the Great Pyramid (National Geographics) - When ancient architects completed construction on the Great Pyramid at Giza, they left behind the greatest riddle of the engineering world how did builders lift limestone blocks weighing an average of two and a half tons, 480 feet up onto the top of the pyramid? For centuries, adventurers and Egyptologists have crawled through every passageway and chamber of the Great Pyramid, measuring and collecting data in an attempt to determine how it was built. For the first time, a revolutionary theory argues that the answer may be inside the pyramid. Architect Jean-Pierre Houdin has devoted his life to solving this mystery by creating incredibly accurate blueprints of the Great Pyramid, using cutting-edge 3-D software.

Gary J. Rose, Ph.D.

Unlocking the Great Pyramid follows Houdin and renowned Egyptologist Bob Brier in Giza as they put Houdins theory to the test.

Stand and Deliver - this true-life story Jaime Escalante, a Los Angeles high school teacher who drives his students on to excellence by teaching them A/P calculus.

Dangerous Minds - Top Hollywood star Michelle Pfeiffer (I AM SAM, WHAT LIES BENEATH) is the driving force behind this gripping and uplifting smash hit! Based on an incredible true-life story -- Pfeiffer is former U.S. Marine LouAnne Johnson, a first-time high school teacher assigned to a class of tough but smart inner-city students. When conventional methods fail to reach them, the feisty Ms. Johnson tries the unconventional -- defying the rules and creating her own curriculum! In the process, she instills a new self-confidence in her students -- motivating them toward their greatest potential. Critically acclaimed and powered by a riveting star performance, DANGEROUS MINDS is hard-hitting, crowd-pleasing entertainment you won't soon forget!

Gridiron Gang - Dwayne "The Rock" Johnson stars in this gritty and inspirational movie based on a true story of a group of teenage delinquents given a second chance to redeem themselves by playing football. Sean Porter (Johnson) is a frustrated juvenile probation officer. Most of the kids in his detention camp are either sent back to prison once they leave or meet a violent end when they return to the streets. Desperately looking for a way to make a difference, he and his co-worker Malcolm Moore (Xzibit, TV's "Pimp My Ride") devise a plan to teach discipline and responsibility through the game of football. But with only four weeks before the start of the season, Porter must overcome insurmountable odds to put together a competitive team. It's a season that will test their minds, spirit, and bodies as Porter teaches his players the principles of good character, strength through resiliency, and genuine respect for one another.

Remember the Titans - Academy Award(R)-winner Denzel Washington (Best Actor, TRAINING DAY, 2001) gives a victorious performance in this stirring and uplifting film. REMEMBER THE TITANS is a rousing celebration of how a town torn apart by resentment, friction, and mistrust comes together in triumphant harmony. The year is 1971. After leading his team to 15 winning seasons, football coach Bill Yoast (Will Patton) is demoted and replaced by Herman Boone (Washington), tough, opinionated, and as different from the beloved Yoast as he could be. How these two men overcome their differences and turn a group of hostile young men into champions, plays out in a remarkable and triumphant story full of soul and spirit. You and your family will never forget the Titans.

Gary J. Rose, Ph.D.

The Ron Clark Story - Best Actor in a TV Movie. Three-time Emmy® Award nominee Matthew Perry (TV's Studio 60 on the Sunset Strip, Friends) delivers a "...tour-de-force performance" (Boston Herald) as real-life inspiration Ron Clark, a passionate and innovative teacher who leaves his small hometown to teach in one of Harlem's toughest schools. But to break through to his students, Clark must use unconventional methods, including his groundbreaking classroom rules, to drive them toward their greatest potential. DVD Features include: "The Teacher Behind the Story:" Ron Clark, Matthew Perry, cast & crew interviews; "Making the Grade:" Ron wins the Disney American Teacher Award!; "Stepping Out of the Classroom:" Ron and students tour South Africa; "Breaking New Ground:" A ground-breaking new school

Lean on Me - Academy Award winner Morgan Freeman stars as "Crazy" Joe Clark, the educator assigned as principal to New Jersey's worst high school, in this uplifting true drama. Upon his arrival at his new post, Joe Clark expels kids, fires teachers and antagonizes parents--and wins the hearts of his students--in an uncompromising quest to provide the quality education they deserve.

Freedom Writers - Academy Award winner Morgan Freeman stars as "Crazy" Joe Clark, the educator assigned as principal to New Jersey's worst high school, in this uplifting true drama. Upon his arrival at his new post, Joe Clark expels kids, fires teachers and antagonizes parents--and wins the hearts of his students--in an uncompromising quest to provide the quality education they deserve.

Rudy - All his life, people have told Rudy he's not good enough, not smart enough, not big enough. But nothing can stop his impossible dream of playing football for Notre Dame. From the time he's a young boy, Rudy (Sean Astin) is determined to join the Fighting Irish. But his blue-collar family only laughs at his ambitions - they know Rudy will follow his father and brothers to the local steel mill. And, for four long years after high school, he does just that. But some dreams won't die, as Rudy proves when he goes to heroic, occasionally hilarious, lengths to win admission to Notre Dame. Once there, he becomes a walk-on player, serving as little more than a human tackling dummy against the starting players. Bloodied but unbeaten, Rudy wins the respect of legendary coach Ara Parseghian and the other Irish players, who give him one shot at gridiron glory. An incredible true story from the creators of Hoosiers, RUDY is an unforgettable testament to the power of dreams and the triumph of the commitment.

Radio - For anyone who ever had a dream and everyone with the courage to stand up for what they believe, comes the real-life story of Robert "Radio"

Kennedy. Experience Radio's journey from a man no one understands to the coach no one could live without. Together with Head Coach Harold Jones, Radio inspired a football team to become champions and a town to open their hearts. Heroic performances from Academy Award Winner Cuba Gooding, Jr. and Academy Award Nominee Ed Harris will have you laughing, crying and cheering for the man who proved, the world's greatest victories happen in real life.

Life of a King - LIFE OF A KING is the true story of one man's inspiring mission to better the future of inner-city youth in Washington, D.C. After being incarcerated for 18 years, Eugene Brown (Academy Award®-winner Cuba Gooding Jr.) established the Big Chair Chess Club to help pull kids off the streets. Using the simple chess-inspired motto "think before you move," Brown helped give troubled students something that he never had: a future.

The Great Escape - A stirring example of courage and the indomitable human spirit, for many John Sturges's *The Great Escape,* is both the definitive World War II drama and the nonpareil prison escape movie. Featuring an unequalled ensemble cast in a rivetingly authentic true-life scenario set to Elmer Bernstein›s admirable music, this picture is both a template for subsequent action-adventure movies and one of the last glories of Golden Age Hollywood. Reunited with the director who made him a star in *The Magnificent Seven,* Steve McQueen gives a career-defining performance as the laconic Hilts, the baseball-loving, motorbike-riding "Cooler King." The rest of the all-male Anglo-American cast--Dickie Attenborough, Donald Pleasance, James Garner, Charles Bronson, David McCallum, James Coburn, and Gordon Jackson--make the most of their meaty roles (though you have to forgive Coburn his Australian accent). Closely based on Paul Brickhill's book, the various escape attempts, scrounging, forging, and ferreting activities are authentically realized thanks also to technical advisor Wally Flood, one of the original tunnel-digging POWs. Sturges orchestrates the climax with total conviction, giving us both high action and very poignant human drama. Without trivializing the grim reality, *The Great Escape* thrillingly celebrates the heroism of men who never gave up the fight. *--Mark Walker*

Rose Red (Based on Stephen King Novel)

The story (about a researcher into the paranormal who takes a team of psychics into a haunted house) recycles themes that King has used before--a telekinetic girl, a house with its own consciousness--but for his fans, the familiarity is probably comfortable and even enjoyable. The cast (including Nancy Travis, Julian Sands, and Melanie Lynsky from *Heavenly Creatures*) give committed performances, and the special effects are television-grade but used pretty well. Most of it doesn't make much sense, but at its best *Rose Red* is absurd and creepy at the same time.

Number of discs: 2
Rated: PG-13 Parents Strongly Cautioned
Studio: Lions Gate
DVD Release Date: December 11, 2003
Run Time: 254 minutes

Winchester House Explored: Secrets of the Mansion

In 1884, Sarah Winchester moved out west and purchased an eight-room farmhouse in San Jose, California. And for 38 years, 24 hours a day, craftsmen, artisans and woodworkers were kept busy building (and rebuilding) the most mysterious mansion ever created. Just why did one of the wealthiest women in the United States spend so much time and over five and a half million dollars on her home? Watch this amazing video! You'll be intrigued by the incredible details of Sarah's architectural fantasy, and learn the secrets of this "beautiful but bizarre" 160 room Victorian Mansion. Not only will you see the exquisite master craftsmanship and the beautiful original Tiffany art glass windows, but also the stairways vanishing in mid-flight, doors that swing open to expose... nothing and stair steps each a mere two inches tall!

Rated: NR Number of tapes: 1 Studio: Winchester Mystery House Run Time: 20 minutes

Teaching Material/Exercises/Videos etc.

My list could continue but suffice to say that you must know your students and how best to teach them the material regardless of the discipline. Keep it fresh and relevant. Remember that it is not just a time filler. I generally had to watch the film and decide what type of lesson plan I wanted to construct and how I would assess my students following the viewing.

When it comes to English/Grammar and Essay writing, a lot of motivation is needed to get them started. In grammar, I have experienced that at-risk students, including adults, like to have notes prepared with missing information which I will allude to later in this section. While watching any of the films listed, I had a prepared outline for them to follow. Since my incarcerated students could not have hard-bound books nor be trusted with paperback books, they only had their notes which I allowed them to use during test day. The more complete their notes, the better chance they had on their test. Any disaster DVDs my student had to research and discuss where the film was inaccurate. For example, the movie CORE, or San Andreas.

English - The State of California for many years required high school senior to pass the California Exit Exam. This was in addition to them obtaining the required amount of credits for graduation. Many of my at-risk students were atrocious spellers and requesting them to write a simple one paragraph essay was extremely taxing for them.

One of the exercises I used was bingo games based on antonym, homonyms, correct word usage and finally essay assignments for a small prize. I have found that at-risk students seem to relish competition, so even a small candy bar, or donut, gets their creative juices flowing.

Find a good book or Internet site that requires your students to select the correct word usage. Some even offer crossword puzzles. For example, even my incarcerated adults, studying for their GED love exercises such as:

Do you have a tooth _____? (lose, loose)
Or, _____ the best basketball player I know. (Your, You're).

One morning I brought in my CD player containing the song for Eve of Destruction. I told my students that they would participate in an essay competition with three cash prizes.

First prize winners would receive a $100 pot prize. Second place: $75. Third place: $50. In addition, winners of these three prizes would attend dinner with me at our local Applebee's.

I then explained their assignment. They had to research the meaning the lyrics of the song and then compose a minimum five-paragraph essay grammatically correct for judging. They were given one week to complete the assignment. They could determine the size of their group but had to show the contribution of each member. I pointed out that the more in their group, the less prize money each would receive. Only a few decided to work solo.

Students were given few hours each week to work on their assignment since many did not have computer at home. Even then it was fun watching them protect their research so that a rival group could not "borrow" their stuff.

My teaching assistants did the judging and I waited until a Friday afternoon to reveal the winners on each prize group. My God, they got so excited and clapped for their fellow students who want the prizes. This showed me that we were slowly becoming a family.

My view is that competition is healthy and part of life. Differing from those with the view that "everyone is a winner," I explained to my students that in life, there are winners and losers. Being able to deal when things do not work out as planned, is part of growing into a contributing member of society.

Another example of how my students evolved into respecting each other and accepting accountability for their action, was observed during a football game. My students realized from my day one introduction, that physical education had to be earned by every one: and, one student could ruin it for the rest of the class. Some of my colleagues felt that this was peer pressure and that it had no room in a classroom. Here is how I sold this to my class by use of a football analogy.

A football team is on the one-foot line about ready to score. It is fourth down with no time on the clock. It is now or never for the team, which is a term I used to describe my students in my classroom.

Just before the ball is snapped, one of a lineman jumps offsides. The ball is moved back beyond the 5-yard line making the chance to score harder for the team. I then expanded this thought by placing all of them in two groups of engineers assigned to a top project of a corporation. Whichever team comes up with the best idea for the new item in time and under budget, their team members each receive a $25,000 bonus. Everyone must work together pulling their own load. As can be seen, I have turned a simple unstated rule of showing respect for each other and working together from the classroom to a real-life situation.

A few days before our Thanksgiving break began, I informed that class that we would be having our first every "Turkey Bowl." I selected two of my sergeants who conducted a player draft in the classroom. They were given time to create plays and get organized. On the day of the big game, I showed them a large cake I have prepared by Costco showing a turkey in the center of the cake surrounded by Turkey Bowl.

All my cadets (students) played for the right to be crowned Turkey Bowl champions and take the cake I had purchased. At the end of the game, I called the winning team's captain and team members to the front of the class. I presented their captain and team their hard-earned cake. He gathered his team together into a large huddle. He then asked if he could address the rest of the class. After I gave him permission, he stated that everyone gave their hearts out there on the football field and his team has decided to share 1/3 of the cake with the rest of the class. They had just demonstrated a life skill and did it on their own with no coaching from me.

Teaching Material/Exercises/Videos etc.

Literature – In juvenile hall we lacked any real library and were limited to the availability of good literature books. I contacted Barnes and Noble and worked out a teacher's discount resulting in my purchase of a set of 21 copies of Shakespeare's plays entitle No Fear Romeo and Juliet, Macbeth, Julius Caesar, Hamlet and King Lear. What is great about these books is that on one side of the page is the original Shakespeare wording, while on the right, it is translated to modern English. Example: Shakespeare, *"what light from yonder window breaks."* No Fear translation: "hey, where is that light coming from?" Get your students in the mood by modifying their voices. You should have witnessed my hardcore juvenile delinquents playing the parts of the three witches as they met at the start of *Lady Macbeth*.

I would assign various parts initially, making sure I had a strong reader for those parts requiring such. It was fun assigning female parts to males who were asked to reflect this in their voice. When we got to some of the famous dialog of the plays such as "what light through yonder window break," I would show how the language has changed from Shakespeare time to theirs. It is through these readings and play enactments, that my students were introduced to terms and literary techniques such as foreshadowing, flashbacks, metaphors, similes, and even poetry.

Even though my students had been label "at-risk," I still told them that I would be challenging them by requiring them to read the same material as our top

Gary J. Rose, Ph.D.

traditional high schools. An Internet search listed the required reading of the various grade levels. I selected those literature pieces that I felt they would enjoy. The following is a partial list of the various books were reviewed which were later examined by watching Hollywood rendition of these books.

White Fang – Jack London's classic adventure story about the friendship developed between a Yukon gold hunter and the mixed dog-wolf he rescues for the hands of a man who mistreats him.

The Crucible – Based on the play of Arthur Miller showing how young girls were able to turn the town of Salem into witch-hunts culminating in the Salem Witchcraft trials and executions.

My Side of the Mountain - In 1959, Jean Craighead George published *My Side of the Mountain*. This coming-of-age story about a boy and his falcon went on to win a Newbery Honor, and for the past forty years has enthralled and entertained generations of would-be Sam Gribleys.

Treasure Island - is an adventure novel by Scottish author Robert Louis Stevenson, narrating a tale of "buccaneers and buried gold". Its influence is enormous on the popular perception of pirates, including such elements as treasure maps marked with an «X», schooners, the Black Spot tropical islands, and one-legged seamen bearing parrots on their shoulders

Robinson Crusoe - Robinson Crusoe flees Britain on a ship after killing his friend over the love of Mary. A fierce ocean storm wrecks his ship and leaves him stranded by himself on an uncharted island. Left to fend for himself, Crusoe seeks out a tentative survival on the island, until he meets Friday, a tribesman whom he saves from being sacrificed. Initially, Crusoe is thrilled to finally have a friend, but he has to defend himself against the tribe who uses the island to sacrifice tribesman to their gods. During time their relationship changes from master-slave to a mutual respected friendship despite their difference in culture and religion.

Twenty-thousand Leagues Under the Sea - Professor Arronax and Ned Land meet Captain Nemo, who reveals that the so-called sea monster they've been told about is actually his submarine The Nautilus.

The Count of Monte Christo - A young man, falsely imprisoned by his jealous "friend", escapes and uses a hidden treasure to exact his revenge.

Rose Red – Based on the Stephen King novel, A group of people with psychic powers are invited to spend the night in a haunted house.

Gary J. Rose, Ph.D.

Freedom Writers - A young teacher inspires her class of at-risk students to learn tolerance, apply themselves and pursue education beyond high school. Based on the book Freedom Writers Diaries.

Dangerous Minds - A former -Marine turned teacher struggles to connect with her students in an inner-city school. Based on the true story and novel.

Life of a King - Ex-felon, Eugene Brown, establishes a Chess Club for inner city teenagers in Washington, D.C. Based on a true story.

Diary of Anne Frank - ***The Diary of Anne Frank***, is a book of the writings from the Dutch language diary kept by Anne Frank while she was in hiding for two years with her family during the Nazi occupation of the Netherlands. The family was apprehended in 1944, and Anne Frank died of typhus in the Bergen-Belsen concentration camp in 1945. The diary was retrieved by Miep Gies, who gave it to Anne's father, Otto Frank, the family's only known survivor, just after the war was over. The diary has since been published in more than 60 languages.

    An excellent film to show at the conclusion your reading is the film Anne Frank, The life of Anne Frank and her family from 1939 to 1945: pre-war fears, invasion of Netherlands by German troops, hiding in Amsterdam, deportation to the camps, and return of Anne's father.

Teaching Material/Exercises/Videos etc.

Stars: Ben Kingsley, Hannah Taylor Gordon, Tatjana Blacher

Economics: I love all of the "For Dummies" books and have used several of them as source material for my curriculum Teaching economics to a bunch of at-risk high school students is tough and can be extremely boring but I found the Economics for Dummies is an excellent book with great examples that your students can relate too. The economy is always changing but some things are eternal! *Economics for Dummies, Third Edition*, gives you everything you need to understand our rapidly evolving economy as well as the basics that never change. What's the best way to fight poverty? How can governments boost employment and wage growth? What can be done to protect endangered species and the environment?

This book answers all those questions in simple language while tracking with a traditional introductory economics class. Following in the steps of the first and second editions, the thoroughly updated Third Edition is a useful study guide and supplement to any high school or college level economics class.

- Discover the ins and outs of irrational consumers with a new chapter on behavioral economics
- Understand and apply the most powerful tool in economics: the model of supply and demand
- Get help recognizing the causes of recessions and the weapons that governments and central banks use to fight back

Gary J. Rose, Ph.D.

- Understand the origins and aftermath of financial crises
- From this material which I use in my lecture, I create my own quizzes and exams.

U.S. Government: Since my classes contained both middle school and high school at-risk students, I liked to use the Painless Series of books. *Painless American Government* (Painless Series) Paperback – February 1, 2004 is an excellent fun book that conveys everything your students need to know to understand our government and U.S. Constitution. Titles in Barron's Painless series are designed for middle school and high school students, helping them excel in subjects they might expect to be either hopelessly boring or excruciatingly difficult. The authors are all experienced teachers, adept at winning the hearts and minds of adolescents, and skillful in adding a light, humorous touch to even the heaviest and grimmest topics. This book opens with a general description of government and a comparison of democracy as practiced by the founding fathers and how it operates in today's America. The author goes on to discuss the Constitution as our basis of government, civil liberties and civil rights, the legislative, executive, and judicial branches of the federal government, elections and political parties, how public policy is created and shaped, and how each citizen can become involved in the process of self-government. The book includes quizzes with answer keys.

Teaching Material/Exercises/Videos etc.

Art History and Art: Let me say that I am a terrible artist. This skill is possessed by my mom and no one else in my family. However, I am fascinated by the lives and times of famous artists and musicians such as Michelangelo, Raphael, Leonardo DE Vinci, Beethoven, Mozart, Haydn, and many others.

I have prepared PowerPoints that I created of all the individuals cited above. After my class studied Michelangelo, and with permission of the probation staff, the morning before my students arrived in their classroom, I had taped pictures of several of the panels of the Sistine chapel's ceiling, under their desks. I then issued them a counted set of color pens and pencils. Their job, for a cup of coffee, was to lay on the floor under their desk and color in the panels which would be judged by the probation department. It did not take long for complaints to be heard of how their arms ached and asked how could Michelangelo be in this position for so many years.

For Leonardo DE Vinci, I showed them a PowerPoint of his life and finished by showing drawings of his various inventions. I used the same technique for the great composers with the addition of playing their famous pieces.

Most of these teaching aids are still available on various websites and well as Amazon and eBay. There are also many new sites on the web in which fellow educators are sharing some of the material they use in the classroom. Some of this is free, while others charge a fee. Unfortunately, some of the material I used was personally created and therefore I can only articulate what and how I put the material together. If you liked the format and context, I am sure you can put together a more up to date PowerPoint to impress your students.

The teaching aids will correspond with a course of study and I will in some cases explain how I overlap or parlay this into other courses if it is relevant. For example, in literature we may be reading *The Diary of Anne Frank*. From that novel, I talk about the Holocaust and the death camps. I have bridges from literature to U.S./World History. Or, if I am teaching my students (juvenile and adults) interest calculations I then discuss economics and the stock market.

Math:

Basic Math – *No Fear Math – All the Basic* Publisher: Barnes and Nobel Publication, ISBN:2059301328, copyright 2005, (www.sparknotes.com)

This book contains instruction in Addition, Subtraction, Multiplication and Division as well as fractions, factoring, operations and properties, decimals, percentages, exponents and powers, square roots, positive and negative numbers, ratios and proportions, as well as statistics and graphs. At the end of each chapter is a section named simply, *Your Turn* in which approximately 20 problems are used to check your students for comprehension.

Teaching Material/Exercises/Videos etc.

California Mathematics Review II – Publisher: American Book Company (www.americanbookcompany.com) Toll free number: (888) 264-5877, copyright 2007, ISBN: 978-1-59807-071-2

Content: Mathematics Review from 6th grade – Algebra 1. Even more detailed than No Fear Math since it is focused on what a 12 grader need to know to pass the now replace, California Exit Exam with much more practice problems for you students. Much more emphasis on Algebra including systems of equations and inequalities and plane geometry. I used this book to supplement the material I presented to my juvenile and incarcerated adults from the No Fear Math book.

Prior to an upcoming holiday such as Labor Day, Valentine's Day, 4th of July, Halloween, Thanksgiving and Christmas, I would search the web for fun activities such as crossword puzzles or math computations with a holiday theme just as a change of pace. As stated previously, many teachers are willing to share their material on the web and I encourage you to do the same.

No Fear Grammar – Publisher: Barnes and Nobles through Spark notes.

(ISBN:20593013286) copyright 2006. Another of the *No Fear* books that also include if interested, *No Fear Vocabulary*, *No Fear Algebra* and *No Fear Spanish*. Down and dirty grammar review with practical review at the end of each chapter.

Gary J. Rose, Ph.D.

Essential College English: A Grammar, Punctuation, and Writing Workbook (6th Edition by **Norwood Selby** (Author), **Pamela S. Bledsoe** (Author) ISBN-13: 978-0321088307. This is an excellent grammar workbook that provides a complete, clear treatment of the rules of grammar and punctuation. Incorporating a friendly and engaging tone throughout, the author's focus on the traditional principles of basic, sentence-level grammar and usage. Each chapter begins with a practice "Find the Error" activity, progresses to lessons and numerous exercises to reinforce each lesson, and concludes with further Review and Editing Tests to help readers retain what they have learned in each chapter. With journal and writing assignments at the end of each chapter, the book places greater emphasis on writing and the writing process. I use an earlier edition to supplement the *No Fear Grammar* book which I used as an initial presentation.

No Fear Shakespeare Books – Publisher: Barnes and Noble through Spark note. Each *No Fear* guide contains:
- The complete text of the original play
- A line-by-line translation that puts the words into everyday language
- A complete list of characters, with descriptions
- Plenty of helpful commentaries

Most of the famous plays are there (in a separate book); *Romeo and Juliet, Julius Caesar, Macbeth,*

Teaching Material/Exercises/Videos etc.

*Hamlet, The Tempest, Othello, The Merchant of Venice, As You Like It, Twelfth Night, King Lear, He*nry V, *Richard III, A Midnights Summer Dream, Antony and Cleopatra, and the Winter's Tale.* What I enjoyed with these No Fear Shakespeare books was that on one side of the page was the play as written by the famous writer, while on the opposite page was the English translation, sometimes with slang. I used *Romeo and Juliet, Macbeth, Othello,* and *King Lear* with my juvenile delinquents and they loved playing their assigned parts. From a social studies concept, think of the spinoffs you can use from these masterpieces: gangs, hatred, jealousy, envy, lust etc. Also, great material for an essay.

After reading each act, my students took a comprehensive exam which conveniently is already created and available for you to copy and paste on the Spark notes web page: www.sparknotes.com/shakespeare.

Critical Reading Series: Disasters! 1st Edition by Henry Billings (Author), Melissa Billings (Author) ISBN-13: 978-0890611128 ISBN-10: 0890611122 Reading Level 6-8 and Interest Level 6-19 Topics are different for each book such as: Monsters, Phenomena, Calamities and Aliens and UFOs. Great discussion pieces and essay assignment material.

I could go on and on with suggestions about various books/films I have used successfully, but a good teacher should always be on the lookout for the newest items available that can be used in your classroom. Sometimes when introducing a film, a student would inquire if the film is in color or black and white, verbalizing his disdain for the later. That did not mean I would never show a black and white film, it just meant that I had to "charge" my students into why I chose to show them an older film. Most of the time this introduction of the film sufficed them.

For example, teaching so many at-risk juveniles, when I saw the film Gridiron Gang, I quickly monitored when it was going to be available for purchase as a great social studies and social skill film. The Ron Clark film is another example of how film can be effectively used in your classroom to discuss and engage your students.

"How beautiful it is to be silent when someone expects you to be enraged."

TEACHING WITH LOVE AND LOGIC, BEST, PBIS AND NURTURED HEARTS

This chapter will address various classroom management and behavioral modification programs being offered in various school districts throughout the country in hopes of reducing the number of problems a classroom teacher may face.

I was exposed to these programs in this order, B.E.S.T., Nurtured Hearts, PBIS and finally Love and Logic and will use this order to review the basic content and rationale for each. I will admit that of the four, the one that I prefer is Teaching With Love and Logic and found that it seems to use common sense more than the other three. This may be based on what I brought to the teaching profession from my previous career in law enforcement and my psychology background, but more teachers that have struggled with classroom management felt much more comfortable using these techniques.

Burrhus Frederic Skinner (March 20, 1904 – August 18, 1990), commonly known as B. F. Skinner, was an American psychologist and behaviorist. He was the Edgar Pierce Professor of Psychology at Harvard University from 1958 until his retirement in 1974.

Skinner believed that human action was dependent on the consequences of previous actions. In other words, if the consequences for a person's actions are bad, there is a high chance the action will not be repeated; if the consequences are good, the probability of the action being repeated becomes stronger. Skinner called this the principle of reinforcement. To strengthen behavior, Skinner used operant conditioning. To study operant conditioning, he invented the now famous operant conditioning chamber, also known as the Skinner Box. Skinner called his approach to the study of behavior radical behaviorism. He distinguished two sorts of behavior—respondent and operant—which are controlled in different ways. Respondent behaviors are elicited by stimuli and may be modified through respondent conditioning, which is often called "Pavlovian conditioning" or "classical conditioning" in which a neutral stimulus is paired with an eliciting stimulus.

Ivan Pavlov who preceded Skinner, experimented with dogs. He noticed that when his dogs heard sounds of an approaching assistant that normally fed them, that they began to salivate at his approach. Together with operant conditioning, classical conditioning became the foundation of behaviorism, a school of psychology which was dominant in the mid-20th century and is still an important influence on the practice of psychological therapy and the study of animal behavior.

As the first step to his experiment, Skinner placed a hungry rat inside the Skinner Box. After a brief time getting used to his new environment by being inactive, the rat began to explore his new surroundings. Eventually, the rat found a lever and found that after pressing it, a food pellet was released inside the box. After it filled its hunger, it started exploring the box again, and after a while, it pressed the lever for the second time as it grew hungry again. This phenomenon continued for the third, fourth and the fifth time, and after a while, the hungry rat immediately pressed the lever once it was placed in the box. Then the conditioning was deemed to be complete.

Educational researchers decided in my opinion, that if it worked on animals, it could work on students and thus began these behavioral modification programs. After one was introduced, a few years later a second more improved model was introduced and so on. Each (with the exception of Teaching With Love and Logic) shared the common belief that positive reinforcement (rewards for positive behavior) will make a child continue to display the desired behavior a classroom teacher desires. These programs believe that it is the most effective method of shaping behavior because it is the most pleasant. For example, praise and reward are both used in positive reinforcement.

I was introduced to B.E.S.T. training in the 1990s while teaching at our local juvenile detention facility The program was designed to provide quality behavior analytic treatment programs to children with Autism Spectrum Disorders as well as individuals with other developmental disabilities.

Using functional assessments and skill assessments, a teacher tries to determine the reasons/functions/motivation for the individual's behavior. Behaviors often referred for this type of assessment include aggression, noncompliance, and tantrums. According to their literature (http://www.bestforautism.com/services.html) the goal of the **Functional Assessment** is to identify and define undesirable behaviors, identify the times, events, and situations that predict when behavior will and will not occur, determine what results occur and how these results may be maintaining the problem behavior, identify appropriate alternative behaviors, and create goals and develop a plan. Whereas **Skill Assessments** are completed to determine what skills an individual (an infant, toddler, child or adolescent) has or does not have, what skills are most needed, and what strategies, supports, and settings are going to be most beneficial in working towards those skills.

Of course, B.E.S.T. can provide brief or on-going consultation (for a cost) in the areas of:
- Program designs
- Data collection systems
- Treatment strategies
- Behavior support strategies

Gary J. Rose, Ph.D.

Nurtured Hearts (called the Nurtured Hearts Approach) was created by Howard Glasser in the early 1990 and was introduced to our district after B.E.S.T. never really got off the ground. The problem with B.E.S.T. is that in juvenile hall, the wards (juveniles) new the rules and saw first-hand, what the consequences were for not following them. There was always at least one probation officer in the classroom so zero tolerance was the norm for inappropriate behavior. As the only teacher in the classroom, I did not have time to work individually with a person's social skills.

The Nurtured Heart Approach® is a relationship-focused methodology founded strategically in The 3 Stands™ for helping children (and adults) build their Inner Wealth® and use their intensity in successful ways. It has become a powerful way of awakening the inherent greatness in all children while facilitating parenting and classroom success. (http://difficult.com/mother.)

The essence of the Approach is a set of core methodologies originally developed for working with the most difficult children. It has a proven impact on every child, including those who are challenged behaviorally, socially and academically. The Nurtured Heart Approach has been shown to create transformative changes in children diagnosed with ADHD, Oppositional Defiant Disorder, Reactive Attachment Disorder and other behavioral, emotional and anxiety related symptoms – almost always without the need for long-term mental health treatment. Even children experiencing social cognitive challenges, like Autism Spectrum Disorder and Asperger Syndrome greatly benefit from the Approach, reducing the need for traditional mental health and medical interventions.

Similar to B.E.S.T., this training and program did not last long in our district and was soon replaced with P.B.I.S. The reason for glossing over both B.E.S.T. and Nurtured Hearts is due to my lack of actually using their full-blown program since it seemed to us educators that there would soon be a "new and improved' program invented by researchers so stand tuned. Sure enough, Nurtured Hearts was replaced with P.B.I.S. (Positive Behavior Intervention Supports).

(Positive Behavior Interventions and Supports – P.B.I.S) is a behavior management system used to understand what maintains an individual's challenging behavior. People's inappropriate behaviors are difficult to change because they are functional; they serve a purpose for them. These behaviors are supported by reinforcement in the environment. Are you identifying Skinner's research here?

On their webpage (https://www.pbis.org/) you will see that some bureaucrats in Washington bought into this program since it is now funded by the U.S. Department of Education's Office of Special Education Programs (OSEP) and the Office of Elementary and Secondary Education (OESE). The Technical Assistance Center on PBIS supports schools, districts, and states to build systems capacity for implementing a multi-tiered approach to social, emotional and behavior support. The broad purpose of PBIS is to improve the effectiveness, efficiency and equity of schools and other agencies. PBIS improves social, emotional and academic outcomes for all students, including students with disabilities and students from underrepresented groups.

Of course, like all of these programs a teacher must be trained in how to implement the program and then is expected to use this classroom management program in their classroom as well as teaching all of the prescribed courses, administer all state and federal exams, take role, meet with parents, attend PLC (Professional Learning Communities) and on and on.

In a nutshell (and I am sure those that love PBIS will hate this), you have a classroom of say 30 students. "Little Johnny or Susie" are constantly acting out in class. Not paying attention, cross-talking, throwing things, you get it; a problem child.

We were trained to issue tickets like you would purchase at a raffle. At the end of every day, you give your students a reward (ticket). Later you will hold a drawing to see who the lucky person is to review the reward. B.F. Skinner would be so proud.

So let's say that to keep "little Johnny or Susie" in line, that you will distribute a ticket to each student at the end of each day of instruction, except little Johnny or Suzie, they get five tickets. Five tickets (rewards) to everyone else's one ticket.

Now comes the end of the week where we will hold a raffle. Follow me with the math here. Each compliant student has in their possession five tickets that they put in your fishbowl for the drawing. Oops! Johnny or Susie actually have how many? Let's see, they got five tickets a day giving them 25 tickets that they put in the fishbowl. So, if your son or daughter who follows the rules because they were taught to respect others and their teacher, hopes of winning, they are going up against the odds of 25:5 (Johnny/Susie have 25 tickets in the fishbowl and your student has five.

In a 2015 article in The Bakersfield Californian (by Lauren Foremen, January 4, 2015) a survey of local educators gave the PBIS program mixed reviews. In her article, Lauren Foremen's survey found that just as many respondents, 38.2 percent of the 69 who answered, felt that PBIS was not effective at all at improving student behavior as those who think it is somewhat effective.

Seventy-six respondents answered a question about whether PBIS had made school more dangerous for them. Slightly more than 40 percent answered yes it has, compared to 42.1 percent who indicated it hasn't. But many BCSD (Bakersfield) teachers, who make up more than 60 percent of respondents, indicated PBIS has led to restricted consequences for bad behavior and more work for teachers.

Sixty-nine respondents answered a question about the effectiveness of Restorative Justice, and fewer than half described the practice as somewhat or very effective. About 40 percent of respondents indicated it wasn't effective at all, and many survey participants wrote the strategy isn't applicable to their schools.

He is another experience I had with a modified P.B.I.S. reward situation overseen by our BCBA (Board Certified Behavioral Analyst). I was asked to monitor hourly, any outburst by one of our students, but putting a check mark indicating the time, subject being taught, his actions, etc. Mind you, I had 39 students in my class and all were at-risk, many on probation. She wanted me to stop what I was doing and note the above information.

When I gave her the sheet noting several outburst and disruptions, she jumped on the fact that for at least two hours he did not cause any issues. The next day, she brought him a coffee from Starbucks which he drank in front of the other students. What do you think their reactions were?

But it did not stop there. The next week, she brought him a hamburger, shake and fries while the other students had whatever the cafeteria delivery service brought that day. Of course it took some time for me to quiet down the class due to the perceived and actual inequality of rewards/consequence they had witnessed.

When she returned a few days later, I told her of how he acted after she left and while he was eating his burger. He made the statement that most of the class overheard that, "that dumb bitch thinks I am going to change."

Teaching with Love and Logic, BEST, PBIS and Nurtured Hearts

My main bias against these three behavioral modification programs is that they set up the student(s) for failure in the real world. In what job does an employee get a reward at the conclusion of each hour or day? Their reward is a paycheck and hopefully benefits. My students equate a paycheck like their report card. You most likely will receive an evaluation on your work performance and probably a visit to the HR department for inappropriate work-related behavior and I doubt that they will give you a burger, shake and fries if you show improvement the following week.

That is my bias and request that you do an in-depth analysis of these three behavioral programs to see if they might fit with your personality type. If your district mandates you use one of them, sorry, but don't worry since the way things have gone in the past, there will be a new and improved program coming down the pike: and I bet you that it is BEST practice and researched based.

Since I prefer to use common sense in my classroom management and prepare my students for adulthood and employment, I discovered that the closest program reflecting my philosophy and methods of classroom management (including interaction with disruptive students) is exemplified in the Teaching With Love and Logic program.

So, what is Love and Logic as it relates to classroom management? Love and Logic is a philosophy founded in 1977 by Jim Fay and Foster W. Cline, M.D. The

Love and Logic Institute is dedicated to making parenting and teaching, fun and rewarding, instead of stressful and chaotic. They provide practical tools and techniques that help adults/teacher achieve respectful, healthy relationships with their children. And, in my opinion, do so using common sense, not rewards.

The Love and Logic Institute is dedicated to making parenting and teaching fun and rewarding, instead of stressful and chaotic. All of their work is based on a psychologically sound parenting and teaching philosophy.

The principles of Teaching With Love and Logic can be found on their webpage (https://www.loveandlogic.com/educator/what-is-love-and-logic-for-teachers) and are stated here:

1. Respect, appreciation and love prevents potential problems.
   When students feel respected, appreciated and even loved by their teachers, they are far more motivated and cause far fewer problems.
2. Freedom to problem-love and make decisions fosters motivation
   Students are far calmer and more motivated when their teachers allow them to make choices and solve their own problems within limits.
3. Freedom to problem-solve and make decisions fosters motivation.
   Students are far calmer and more motivated when their teachers allow them to make choices and solve their own problems within limits.

4. Freedom to problem-solve and make decisions fosters motivation
   Students are far calmer and more motivated when their teachers allow them to make choices and solve their own problems within limits.
5. Focusing energy on problem prevention is rewarding
   Successful educators focus most of their energy on simple tools for preventing misbehavior or keeping it small...rather than trying to provide consequences for every problem.
6. Showing empathy and compassion is effective
   When consequences are necessary, effective educators provide them with sincere empathy or compassion.

My first experience with Teaching With Love and Logic happened after I took a teaching position at a newly created charter school. My supervisor was aware of my teaching resume but still requested that I attend the in-house training from a trainer trained by the Love and Logic Institute. After several hours of training I realized that I had been doing most of the elements they teach in the program and made many comments to my fellow collogues attending the classes, how well these recommendation work with extreme at-risk and disruptive students including felons and gang bangers.

I highly recommend you purchase the book *Teaching With Love & Logic* by Jim Fay and David

Gary J. Rose, Ph.D.

Funk (ISBN 10: 0-944634-48-6) or (ISBN: 13: 978-0-944634-48-6). The contents of this book should help elevate any new teacher who is dreading their first day of teaching or veteran teachers who have some bad actors in their classroom.

Take a look: Confronting the myth about discipline
          Discipline and Control
          Perception and Behavior
          The Enhancement of Self-Concept
          Shared Control
          Consequences with Empathy
          Styles of Teaching
          Legal Considerations
          Implementing School Discipline
          Classroom Solutions Using Love and Logic

In this book, the founders of Teaching Love and Logic present numerous examples of disruptive students from real life situations and how to diffuse the situation with less stress to you and your students. In my opinion, this should be required reading in our teacher colleges.

"Those who CAN teach. Those who CAN'T, pass laws about teaching."

WHAT IS WRONG WITH OUR SCHOOLS – A COMMENTARY

If you enjoyed my book up to this chapter, I believe I have demonstrated my love and dedication for teaching "at-risk" students, both juveniles and adults. In reminiscing about my employment as a law enforcement officer and transformation into a teacher of "at-risk" incarcerated students, individuals point out the dichotomy that for years I arrested these law violators and placed them in confinement centers. Now, for a period each day, I am incarcerated with them, now motivated in helping to change their lives.

Back under Introduction, I explained my decision on entering the educational field. I could not believe that our students, here in California, were evaluated in the lower quadrant of achievement when compared to the other fifty states. I could not comprehend how this had occurred since during my elementary and high school years, California always scored extremely high in this comparison.

What is Wrong with our Schools – A Commentary

So, what is wrong with our schools?" The simplistic answer to the question, lack of common sense. We have moved to quickly away from traditional, practical experience teaching to a progressive movement that, many times simply based on different ideologies, dismisses previous tried and proven methods of educating our youth.

A new wave of attacks on American student performance has emerged from both liberals and conservatives. These are fueled by a battery of international tests that compare the United States' students to those in the Organization of Economic Cooperation and Development (OECD) countries, as well as several East Asian countries and cities. The results appear to show America falling behind in key subjects.

In a recent article published by The Observer titled: How American Students Truly Rank in International Testing (By **John A. Tures,** 01/15/18), America used to have a superb public school system, but now we trail most countries. In math, we're 38th in the world among developed countries in terms of how 15 year-olds perform. And it's getting worse, not better."

In the same article, Tures added that critics across the ideological spectrum have denounced U.S. education scores. And Obama's Education Secretary Arne Duncan attacked the performance of American students on international tests, even as high school graduation rates rose to their highest level in several decades.

How can our high school graduation rates increase while our student's performances are decreasing?

In a knowledge-based, global economy, where education is more important than ever before, both to individual success and collective prosperity, our students are basically losing ground. Arne Duncan stated in the article that "the hard truth is that the U.S. is not among the top performing OECD nations in any subject tested."

Professor F.H. Buckley is cited in the article that, "We throw more money at our schools than just about any other country, and what do we get? For our K-12 school system, an honorary membership in the Third World."

Instead of debating why we scored so low, or just throwing money at the problem which is the typical solution by politicians, what countries are at the top and how do they educate their children?

American Federation for Teachers leader Randi Weingarten claims that "high-performing nations, such as Japan, Switzerland, Finland and Poland, have more respect for public education and work to give teachers the resources they need to ensure students, particularly those with greater needs, are successful in the classroom."

If this is the case, that citizens of the United States have less respect for teachers that these four top performing countries, it should not surprise us that many prospective individuals initially interest in becoming educators, expect to make little money and feel their profession is scorned by society, even sometimes mocked somewhat by majors in other fields.

Education specialist Diane Ravitch, and others have talked about how private schools may play a greater role in the solution to our failing schools including colleges and universities. Private schools, which are exempt from liberal social engineering courses, are able to adopt the creativity that students really need to succeed in the global market, which is more about innovation and free thinking than memorization of material that can be easily accessed by a computer. More time can be spent of "old school" topics such as math, science, language arts, social studies, World and U.S. history, U.S. government and citizenship.

One of the problems with public education is, unlike France where a centralized ministry of education governs schools directly, in the U.S., all 50 states maintain authority over public education. And across those 50 states, roughly 13,000 districts shape much, possibly even most, of what happens in local schools.

A second problem is that although most states often take similar approaches to curricula and teacher licensure, they tend to differ considerably in policy and practice. Things like early-childhood education, charter-school regulation, sex education, arts programs, teacher pay, and teacher evaluations are anything but uniform across the 50 states.

It's longstanding American practice for cities and towns to have a significant amount of power over education. But local control also persists because of the importance of context. What schools need in order to succeed depends significantly on the needs and concerns of the local community, and policy tends to reflect that. Teacher hiring, for instance, is usually done at the local level and is often shaped only indirectly by state policy. As a result, the process looks quite different from place to place depending on the approaches districts take to recruiting teachers, screening applicants, and making job offers. Further, while curriculum standards are shaped by states, districts determine what they actually look like and which books students carry around.

Education Week (January 26, 2018), commentator Matthew Lynch, had his previously posted opinion blog on edweek.org from a few years ago in which listed the 10 (More) Reasons Why the U.S. Education System Is Failing, reposted. His list—which addressed economic shortfalls, gender and racial disparities, parent engagement, and more, still persist today with not much progress being seen. Since he felt that the list still ring true, he added 10 additional emerging problems and issues with our education system.

It is very interesting to compare what Mr. Lynch's listed as problems in education in his previous postings (*Education Week*, August 27, 2015 9:43 AM and what he posted in 2018.

2015
1. Parents are not involved enough
2. Schools are closing left and right.
3. Our schools are overcrowded
4. Technology comes with its downsides
5. There is a lack of diversity in gifted education
6. School spending is stagnant, even in our improving economy
7. There is a lack of teacher education innovation
8. 80 percent of students are graduating high school...yet less than half of these students are ready for what's next.
9. Some students are lost to the school-to-prison pipeline
10. There is a nationwide college-gender gap, and surprisingly, we are not focusing on it.

2018
1. In this digital age, we need to rethink literacy
2. The way we currently assess students is not working.
3. We do a poor job of educating boys of color.
4. We continue to retain and socially promote students
5. Anti-intellectualism and academic disengagement are running rampant.
6. We need more year-round schools
7. We are not able to consistently produce quality teachers.

8. We are not doing enough to foster digital equity.
9. We are not doing enough to get girls involved with STEM
10. Teacher-preparation programs don't teach neuroscience.

Has there been a noticeable improvement in most of these cited "problems?" In my opinion, minimal at best.

Do you know the difference between an "old school" and a "new school" classroom? It isn't the one room building still only seen in period dramas in advanced countries.

Do you know the difference between teaching "old school" versus "new school?" In her journal posting, Ann Luther (Luther, A. (2000). The "Old" Method of Teaching Vs. the "New" Method of Teaching. *Journal of Thought, 35*(2), 59-69. Retrieved from http://www.jstor.org/stable/42589616) describes the difference between the two as follows:

In the "old school", the teacher stands in front of the students and presents the material they are to learn. It is the teacher who is responsible to determine what to teach and how to present the material. Students are individually responsible for understanding the material. Students compete for their grades demonstrating their competence. The teacher is viewed as an authority figure.

What is Wrong with our Schools – A Commentary

An educational movement began in the 1970s towards collaborative learning with studies showing signs that there was a positive effect when students studied in small groups. This took place both at the elementary and secondary school levels. The theory was that small group learning held individuals accountable for the group's success and generally increased achievement and improved social skills. This is part of the same philosophy grounded in the new Common Core movement.

Further, it was felt that in small groups, students are "doing" versus memorization and rote understanding of the problems they work on. This method of teaching began to erode the traditional role of the teacher to more of a collaborator – an enabler – a facilitator.

I believe that very few would question the importance of the development of higher-order thinking that the "new school" is implementing, but my observations are that the teacher begins evaluating not the competency of an individual student, the group itself.

Additionally, I have witnessed many small group exercises, in which the alpha male or female, takes over leadership for the group and any introverted students all them to dictate the way the group goes. This of course, will occur generally after the alpha male/female has demonstrated their mastery of the course material.

"At-risk" students, especially those who do not want to apply themselves are eager and quite willing to sit back and let someone else do the work, especially if h/she receives a high-earned grade earned by the group.

Don't misunderstand: I have had my students participate in small group exercises with a lot of success as I monitored each group closely to make sure everyone is participating. But these small group exercises start after I have lectured them the subject matter so that they have the lower-level information upon which to build on. I strongly believe in the Socratic method of teaching especially with my experience of teaching thusly at the college and university level. The teacher is the student's guide to the discipline and as such should show competency and lead.

An "at-risk" teacher, whether the student is a juvenile or adult, must be aware if their student(s) begin to struggle if the material is too rigorous so that they do not give up. Instead a teacher must cooperate with their students without negating the teacher's responsibility to challenge said students.

If a teacher allows students to desire an easy grade, then the teacher has let the student down in h/her further development as a learner. Small group learning must not replace individual learning.

In his book, *The Padeia Proposal* by Mortimer Adler (1982) he and his associates identified the three major areas of language, literature, and fine arts; mathematics and natural sciences, history, geography, and social studies as **crucial** to a twelve-year program of schooling. For them, these three main areas of knowledge "*comprise the most fundamental branches* *of learning and provide the learner with indispensable knowledge about nature and culture, the world in which we live, our social institutions, and ourselves"* (Adler 1982, pp.23-24).

Unfortunately, what I have seen over the past 20+ years is that many school districts allow emphasis on community building and self-esteem to lead them to neglect a curriculum that focuses on specific content and skills. This is also related to a move away from Constructivism – that people learn best when they can relate new information to something with which they are already familiar. I am sure that you, the reader, is probably thinking that everyone knows that and that it is common sense for a student to have a reference that is understood and a foundation that can be built on. But this is not happening in our schools, sadly at all levels.

The educational progressive movement poses that there are no absolutes in a constructivists perspective – in other words, why have our students learn facts, when facts are open to interpretation. Why have students learn facts, when they can "construct" their own interpretation? What do we have after this transformation takes place? The classroom, in my opinion becomes a social laboratory that starts breaking down our traditions, morals, and values.

It is easy for me to agree with one aspect of the new "constructivist claim" that learning must be an active process, but as Robert Marzano (2003, 108), stated as a warning, *"this principle is frequently over-generalized to mean that teachers should rarely (if ever) teach content to students."* He went on to state that *constructivist models of instruction, naively or mistakenly applied, undermine proven teaching practices and unwisely replace them with practices that discourage the mastery of specific and necessary content that secures the correct understanding of the subject matter."*

For me, I can still remember starting each school day standing for the Pledge of Allegiance. We always made sure that our demeanor showed respect for our teachers. We had fifty-minutes courses in English (grammar, literature, penmanship), mathematics, science, world and U.S. history, current events, and physical education.

Today, many classrooms do not even display a U.S. flag must less cite the Pledge of Allegiance. Most students do not receive course material in what we use to term civics. While polling my adult inmates when I taught the social studies content for the GED, less than 1% in each of my classes knew the three branches of government; why the Founding Fathers put in the electoral college; nor what countries did the United States fight in World War II.

This topic will continue to be debated by intellectuals who have never stepped into a classroom especially one containing criminals. Research films and think tanks will diagnosis all of the various issues and issue a report that someone will pay for since it offers all the solutions to the problem. But, has anyone asked the teachers? The ones on the firing line each

What is Wrong with our Schools – A Commentary

and every day. The individuals who are expected by some parents to not only educate their children but teach them social skills and God help you if you dare give their little Johnny or Susan a grade lower than their expectations.

Just a random computer search of various blogs in which teachers were asked what the problem is with our schools offers a plethora of complaints regarding this question (top cited):

1. A lack on the part of the school district to try anything new. Students come to school in the dark, tired and not ready to study. Why can't the school district start school later?
2. Adoption of new programs ("flavor of the month") so quickly before a chance is given to see if the previous programs were working. Not to mention the costs of the new programs and teacher training time.
3. Keep adopting and dumping disciplinary policies and models so fast that teachers have literally no what the current policy is and don't trust administration to follow any policy anyway.
4. Due process by unions preventing the removal of bad teachers. Districts have a process to get rid of a bad teacher but are afraid to proceed.
5. Teachers don't get to teach – they instead spend 60% of their time grading papers, administering state/federal exams, attend IEPs, 504, PLC meeting and behavioral modification training.

6. Parents who should never have been parents.
7. The Common Core Controversy
8. Federal vs. State vs. Local control of schools
9. Push by progressives for differentiation learning – but where will the time, training money, and staff come from?
10. Poor teacher pay with what we put up with in the classroom.
11. Teaching's lack of a central voice.
12. Politicians and "educational experts" always putting in their two-cents.
13. The point of decision making about curriculum, methodology and especially evaluation of students has been moved too far from the classroom.
14. We have fallen to the sales pitches of mega-companies that make a fortune creating "research based" exams, curricula, books and learning material.
15. Lack of administration disciplining students
16. Safety in the classrooms.
17. Class sizes too large.
18. Influx of non-English speaking students

I am closer to the end of my career than the beginning so for those new to the profession, let your dedication and love for teaching shelter you somewhat to all of the problems cited. With fondness, I remember a college professor (retired FBI agent) explain to use during the protests that were taking place on college campus regarding the Vietnam conflict. He said that when society's actions swing too far to the right, we have something like Nazi Germany. If society goes too far to the left, we have anarchy. Using this analogy, education reformers need to return to the middle ground.

My mother, father, brother, sister, relatives and friends were all products of "old school" teaching and even today, with some of them elderly, they can still do math problems, cite the Pledge of Allegiance, tell you how the United States was founded, explain many of the 10 amendments to the U.S. Constitution, discuss the two World Wars, understand the importance of voting, and show respect to those that they disagree with. Not bad for a bunch of "old school" graduates.

SUGGESTIONS

As promised, here are some suggestions you might consider when teaching your "at-risk" students. This, will pertain primarily to your juvenile students since it will address how I taught core high-school subjects. Later, I will cover how I teach my adult inmate students in preparation for their GED examinations. You may see some duplicity in this chapter dealing with the use of movies and DVDs.

Mathematics:

After a quick assessment of my students, I normally start with basic math very similar to what I use with my adult students. I start with multi-column addition problems in which they must demonstrate how to "carry" a number. In subtraction, I wanted to make sure they understood the principle of borrowing. Once I am satisfied in their mastery of addition and subtraction, it is onto to multiplication and division moving from the simple to more complex problems.

Knowing that they understand adding, subtracting, multiplying and division, we move onto decimals. I have found over the years, that students, both juveniles and adults, start to struggle with long division and this is especially true while explaining how to divide

Suggestions

decimals when the divisor has a decimal. In addition, you will have to spend time with many students explaining about the placement of the decimal point after completing multiplication.

Addressing the multiplication of decimals, I instruct all my students to disregard initially, the placement of decimal and to instead just complete the multiplication. Once that is complete, they I show they how to count the numbers to the right of the decimals which tells them how where to now place the decimal point. All of the books I have earlier listed do an excellent job of explaining all of the steps.

The teaching of fractions always seems to be tough on many "at-risk" students both juvenile and adult. It is no wonder why many students get "turned off to math" when this section of math is introduced. Since my career as a teacher started in juvenile hall, I thought that perhaps it was due to their criminal background that they did not comprehend what fractions are nor how they are used in real-life situations. Later, while teaching at a charter school, even many of my high school student struggled with fractions.

I first explain that a fraction is "part of a whole," like percentages. I then draw a picture of a pizza on the whiteboard. I use different color markers adding drawings of mushrooms, onion, pepperoni, sausage, linguica (I'm Portuguese so my pizza must have linguica) – a combination pizza. I divide the pizza down the middle with a black marker and erase half of the pizza, commenting on how good it tasted. I ask my students, how much pizza is left. "A half, they shout out." Good is say, as I take my black marker and divide the half into fourth's. I then ask one of the students if they are hungry and after getting their "yes" answer, erase a quarter (1/4) of the pizza. I again as the class, "How much is left?" One-fourth they will shout out.

Ok, you have just seen a "real-life" demonstration of how fractions are a part of our life. Working backyards I draw another "pizza" and, without filling it in with "goodies", tell them that unless someone takes a slice of the pizza, it represents one whole pizza. Then I divide the pizze into halves, then thirds, then fourths and so on.

To keep their interest, I tell them a story of "Tyler" who I had numerous times as a student housed in juvenile hall. Tyler was a classroom disturber. He always tried to impress the other students that he was tough. Barely reaching five feet, Tyler would wait until he was sure that a probation officer was watching, and then quickly lung out at the biggest student is class and hit him, knowing that probation would intervene so that the bigger student could not retaliate and "kick his butt."

Tyler could not grasp the concept of fractions, so, with permission of the probation staff, I arrangement with our local Round Table Pizza to have them make up four large pizzas. I had them cut the pizzas up into 1/10, 1/16, 1/20 and 1/30 pieces. When the students entered the classroom, the pizza boxes were closed but outside I had the fractions the pizzas were cut into written down.

Suggestions

Tyler was the first person I asked if he would like a piece of pizza. All the other students were told to stay quiet while he made his selection (or they would be moved from the classroom). Tyler, who never paid attention regarding the relationship between the numerator or the denominator, chose, you guessed it, a slice of the pizza cut up into 30 pieces (1/30). I go a piece of pizza, put it on a paper plate and gave it to Tyler. Quickly I asked one of my brightest students what slice of pizza he would like. "I will take a slice of pizza Mr. Rose, from the box of 1/10 please."

You can imagine the Tyler's shock when he saw the difference in sizes\ of the pizza he selected (1/30) compared to other slice (1/10). You would be wrong if you thought that Tyler now got it, but you would be wrong. He continued to try and disrupt the class, but I was ready for him and so was probation.

After the rest of the students got their slice of pizza, there was still a lot left of the 1/20 and 1/30 variety. Once again I asked Tyler if he would like two pieces of 1/30 pizza or two pieces of the 1/20. He chose two slices of the 1/30. On cue, one of the probation officers and I examined the box where the pizza was cut into 1/20 and found eight slices left. We split those slices between ourselves with Tyler shocked on how he lost out again.

Plan to spend a considerable amount of time focused on fractions. For some reason, and I suspect teachers not being properly trained in mathematics (specifically fractions) have promoted many of their students without mastering this important part of math.

I start out explain what is a fraction, improper fraction, and mixed number. I move on to simple addition, subtraction of fractions and mixed numbers, how to reduce fractions, how to convert mixed numbers into improper fractions and vis versa.

Teaching multiplication of fractions first is generally easier for most students to comprehend before introducing the steps of dividing fractions. I start out with common fraction problems such as ½ + ¼ and do the same with subtraction. Then I introduce borrowing and carrying and mixed numbers, always making sure they reduce their answers.

Once I am comfortable with this mastery of the above, I move on to the steps required in dividing fractions. I joke about being old and how, as a teenager, there was a serial on television called *Lost in Space*. I talk about the robot who was always looking out for Will Robinson. When danger was approaching, he would throw out his arms and state, "Danger Will Robinson, Danger!"

I inform them that I want them to think of this image as well as the sign normally placed on a bottle of poison. (skull and crossbones), all equating to DANGER! Every time they see a division sign with fractions, they should pause and think danger because there is an extra step when dealing with these types of problems.

Suggestions

To demonstrate I write on the board ¼ x ¼ = I do the calculations and display the answer.

Then I write ¼ divided by ½ using the appropriate division sign. I start to solve the problem but explain that I see the danger sign and know that while dividing fractions, I must turn the problem into a multiplication problem and invert the second fraction. What I say is, "Danger, danger, (while pointing to the division sign). I then rewrite the first fraction, and say, "I must now blow up the division sign, turning it into a multiplication sign and the force of the explosion, flips the other fraction upside down." Sounds corny but it really works.

Of course, you must also introduce cross-multiplication and the ever present must to reduce or simplify. These strategies are reinforced with daily worksheets and the weekly quiz.

Next up is percentages, discounts, determination of tips, and commissions. Sometimes I will create worksheets in which I will use actual student names in word problems so that they can see the relevance of knowing how to deal with percentages etc. I also introduce a square (see diagram) to help them dissect word problems that ask them to determine the percent, the part, the whole.

Percent Proportion

$$\frac{percent}{100} = \frac{part}{whole}$$

$$\frac{60}{100} = \frac{3}{5}$$

Gary J. Rose, Ph.D.

I typically lecture the strategies for each type of math problem followed by issuing a worksheet for my students to work on which I collect for assessment. This also keeps them honest since each student must turn in their paperwork. Being old school, I also require them to show not only their work, but also require to re-check to see if their answer is correct. This will later be reinforced when I discuss the rules of opposites.

Say I assign a problem of 50 divided by 2.5. Once they do the division calculation, I then require them to use the opposite of division (multiplication) to prove their answer. It really re-enforces their understanding of this rule.

Remarkably, many of my adult inmates do not understand the concept of a number line. I could be related that they never went to school, or just did not pay attention on those rare occasions when they did attend.

Since most my "at-risk" juvenile students are males, I like to use football to explain the number line. My females students seem to like the demonstration. Drawing a "not-to- scale" football diagram on the whiteboard, I pick on a popular male (or female) and name them the quarterback of a team. I place the "ball" on the 30-yard line and have the quarterback complete a pass to another student for "gain" of 15 yards. I draw the football at the site of the completion. Then, under the diagram of the football field, on a number line, I show the addition of +15 to the original

Suggestions

starting position of +30, showing that the ball is now on the 45-yard line.

You guessed it, the next play our quarterback is sacked -10 yards and again, on the football field, I move the football back and again show this move on the number line. Once that I see my students comprehending how to use the number line I erase the football field and number line and draw a line vertically on the board with measurements going up and down from zero. I label it as a weather thermometer and list a few temperature readings. Those weather readings above zero and place on the vertical number line, and negative reading are shown going in the opposite directions.

Another confusing by both my juvenile and adults "at-risk" students is the understanding of absolute values, especially when there is a negative sign in front of the absolute value. The basic math book I listed does an excellent job explaining the concept of absolute values.

Next up are the rules when dealing with exponents. To introduce this section, I write a lareg 2 on the board with a small 4 (exponent) above it. Several students will shout out an incorrect answer of 8. I then make a sound like an incorrect buzzer going off and say, "Thank you for playing, come back next time and play again."

I identify the name of the large two calling it the Base Number. The smaller 4 is the exponent or powers. To help them remember that the answer could never be 8, I draw four small "legs" under the number 2. Below each leg I place a 2 – four times like this: (2)(2)(2)(2). "In Algebra, this is one way of showing multiplication. So, please multiply these twos and tell me what you get." "Sixteen some will shout out." I tell them that they are correct and then put another problem on the board such as 4 to the 3rd. You will still get someone to say, "twelve." Thank them for playing and draw three little legs under the 4 and show this as (4)(4)(4) = They will probably never do this on a test, but they will recall how you taught them.

Positive and negative numbers are introduced by me playing the part of Jaime Escalante in the famous film *Stand and Deliver*, where Escalante points to to the blackboard where he has written a problem the problem +1 + -1 = ? Then he asks his students how many of them have ever gone to the beach and played in the sand. Taking his hand, he asks, as he mimics the scooping of a handful of sand out of the ground. He then states, "This represents a positive; the hole is the negative. How much then do you have when you add a negative one to a position one?" This concept will later be re-emphasize when I show them the film.

I then tell them how Escalante had his students clap while stating, "A positive times a positive, is a positive. A positive times a negative, is a negative. A negative times a positive is a negative. A negative times a negative is a positive." Four simple rules to memorize when multiplying or dividing positive and negative numbers.

Then I tell them that with me, they will only have to remember two rules, not four like Jaime Escalante. Those rules are again for dealing with the multiplication and division of signed numbers. They are: When the signs are the same, the answer is always positive. When the signs are different, the answer is always negative. That's it. Simple.

I issue a work sheet starting with simple adding and subtracting positive and negative numbers, followed by multiplication and division of same signed numbers. Moving from there and referring to "my" two rules on the board about the signs being the same and the signs being different, I assign problems where they must decide if the answer is positive or negative.

Algebra is introduced by my comment that this type of math is really lazy man's math where we use letters to represent a quantity. I ask how many letters there are in our alphabet and wait for an answer. Twenty-six, that is correct, I say. That means that we could have 26 letters (called variable) in our Algebra problems.

I write a very simple Algebra problem on the board: $x + 2 = 4$. Immediately you will students shout out the answer of two. I acknowledge that they got it right and say, "Hey, you guys and gals can already do Algebra." Then I say, "In Algebra, whatever you do on one side of an equation, you must do on the other side." I take a marker and balance it on my finger. I ask the students, why does the marker stay balanced? After getting their answers, I take out my set of keys which are attached to a ring. I slowly slide the ring of keys to one side of the marker and release it, thus causing the marker and keys to hit the floor. "Why did this happen? I ask. You will receive various answers that one side weighs more than the other etc. Then I asked what would happen if I was able to release two identically weighted sets of keys on opposite sides of the marker. They always get the answer correct.

All Algebra is, I tell them, is the use of adding, subtracting, multiplying and dividing at a differently level with addition rules. I draw a checkers board on the whiteboard. I place "checkers" of red and black circles on the board. After asking how many know how to play checkers, I ask them to teach me, but I stress I want to make the first move. I erase a checker from the back row and erase their checker on their back row and say, "King me."

Be prepared for their verbal, "Hey, you can't do that!"

"Why not," I ask.

"Because you can't jump all of those spaces" they respond.

"Oh, you mean there are rules to playing checkers?"

They will know where you are going. I then hit them with a question inquiring how many of them have played chess? "Which is easier to teach, checkers or chess? Receiving their answer of "chess," I ask why?

Because there are different pieces and each can only move certain ways."

"Got it," I respond and add, "Algebra is that same. It is a game with many different rules, but if you understand the rules, just like checkers and chess, you will become good at it."

I ask them to recite for me the "rule of opposites," the two rules when multiplying or dividing signed numbers, after which I write the letters PEMDAS. "Your first three rules you need to know to solve Algebra problems.

PEMDAS is a way of remembering the order of operation or, if you like, the steps or progressions in Algebra to solve a problem. The P stands for Parenthesis, E, stands for Exponents, M, stand for Multiplication, D, stands for Division, A, stands for Addition, and S, stands for Subtraction. A simple statement of Please Excuse My Dear Aunt Sally will help them remember, but since I had/have hardcore criminals as students, in the hall they changed it to "**P**lease **E**xcuse **M**y **D**umb **A**ss **S**ister." Hey, whatever helps them remember the Order of Operations. Worksheets after worksheets are worked on until you progress to the more complex Algebra problems, encouraging them all the time that we will now learn a new rule etc.

Economics:

I used the books listed in chapter 12 when teaching economics. Even though, at the time in California, economics was only required of 12th-graders, I felt that all of my students, being in the same classroom, could benefit from knowledge of economics. Two exercised that worked well for me was an assignment where, at Christmas time, I asked my students to develop a new toy to be sold. They had to estimate the cost of production (overhead), marketing, packaging etc. You will be surprised at the effort put into this project by your "at-risk" students. Make sure you tell them that whatever they plan to create has to be legal.

Two of my hardcore students at juvenile hall first came up with a survey that they requested the female wards would complete. Examining the survey, both probation and I, along with the female teacher in the girls unit, gave the survey to the female students. Satisfied with their survey results, the two students went to work. They even created a business plan.

What did they "invent?" While, this toy has been on the market for years, but sadly it created and copyrighted by someone else and they never got credit for it. They created a computer game targeting young girls who attend slumber parties. The partygoers would use a game provided camera and take a picture of each other. That picture was downloaded and upon appearing on the screen, the partygoers could add makeup, earrings, different hair styles etc. The survey they conducted with the girl's unit, confirmed that there would be a target audience interested in buying their game.

One whole day at juvenile hall was set aside for each team to present their business plan, costs, profit/loss margin, producing drawings and renditions of what their idea would look like. Probation was very impressed.

Suggestions

The second exercise I used being a former stockbroker, was a lecture on investment basics. My students learned what was a stock, bond, mutual fund, risk/reward, bull vs. bear, money market funds, dollar-cost averaging, 401k plans, IRAs, and the overview of the stockmarket. Then, I would open a small account using my brokerage firm and split the class up into groups whose job was to use the Wall Street Journal and select several stocks that I would purchase and watch advance or decline during the week. They loved seeing "their" money grow and yelled at each other when "their" stocks were heading in the wrong direction.

World and U.S. History:

For over 15 years, I have classes in which my student population consisted of a mix of
7th-through 12th-graders, making it hard to follow the state mandated curriculum, especially since I was generally the only teacher of up to 42 students. Instead, I chose to teach all of them what an 9th-grader through 12th-grader must know before taking and passing the non-defunct California High School Exit Exam.

I started with World History focusing on ancient civilizations such as the Greeks, Romans, Egyptians. I added on all the main events during this time-period using PowerPoints I purchased from Multimedia

Learning (http://multimedialearning.org/) I created my own "fill-in the blanks" worksheets and while lecturing, my students had to place the missing word, phase in the space provided. I told them that in college, they would be responsible to not only listen to their professor, look at his/her PowerPoint as well as take notes, so I wanted them to experience this first in my classroom.

Using the timeframe of World War I, I used that as the time that I would take a pause from World History and begin U.S. history, starting with the Vikings and moving to the colonies. Advancing from the Revolutionary War to the event leading to World War I, the two "histories" became one. More global lectures begin in which I would talk about events in the world and it's impact on the United States and vis versa. Again, I cannot stop complimenting the job Multi-Media Learning has to offer in these regards.

Around the holidays, regardless of what point I was in history, I would take time to explain the origins of Halloween, Thanksgiving, Christmas as well as Pearl Harbor, 9-11 and other historical events both here and abroad. (See list of DVDs in earlier chapters). You can always ask you students to write essays on these subjects. For example, before I showed them the film *Flight 93)* I read to them some of the stories from loves one who recall the last conversations they had with the passengers onboard this doomed flight. I asked my students to think and then write, about what they would say if they were one of these passengers. Be prepared to read some powerful letters.

Suggestions

English/Grammar/Literature

Let me be upfront. I find grammar very boring, so I heavily relied on the books I have listed earlier. I used these books, and sources on-line) to create my own lesson plans. My worksheets allowed my students to circle the correct verb tense, contractions, editing errors and then I always had to write a five-paragraph essay. I also used the bingo games listed in this book and had small prizes for those that won. Synonyms, Antonyms, Prefixes and Suffixes bingo games are a hit and these games are still available for purchase. Watch out for cheaters.

I assigned research papers on various subjects. It might simply be having your "at-risk" students research their future career. Have them write to agencies, for example the F.B.I. and see what the qualifications are to become an agent. Make them go to a plumbing firm and inquire about the skills and pathways that should be taken to become a plumber etc. The key is to make if fun and relevant to them.

Literature can be fun and rewarding. I always tried to make it a requirement for my students to have a "free-reading" book handy in case they complete their assignment before others. Later I purchased the *No Fear Shakespeare* books and we, as a class, acted out the plays. In the hall, we even went further and, with the help of my teaching assistant who went to a thrift shop and got a lot of clothing, put on a play for the younger wards of the hall.

I would also purchase classical books such as Robinson Crusoe, the Count of Monte Christo, and others, and after having my class finish the book (and accompanying quizzes that I created), we would watch the latest Hollywood version and critic how it compared to the book.

As stated earlier in this book, I would also hold essay contests with cash prizes and a dinner night out with yours truly. Only two people could work together on the essay assignment, but be aware of some lazy students just going along for a ride and not producing any work.

While on the subject of awards, I bought certificates from Jones School Supply (https://wwe.jonesawards.com) who have a great selection awards from paper certificates to trophies. "At-risk" student may act tough, but they cannot wait to see their papers displayed on the walls of your classroom under a job well done sign.

Essay Writing:

Many students, even though who are not labeled "at-risk", hate to write. And, if they do, it will generally appear as text messages like they do on their cell phones. Gone are the days in education, where penmanship and cursive writing is part of the English curriculum.

Yet, many examinations such as the GED English/Grammar, and many college and universities entrance

Suggestions

exams/applications, require a student to be able to construct at least a five-paragraph essay. Teaching "old school" style, I require all my students to have this ability, and taught them the different types of essays: Narrative, Descriptive, Expository and Persuasive. On the GED examination, they must have this ability.

After a few weeks reviewing common grammar errors, I introduce them to what I call the "Bubble Method" of constructing a five-paragraph essay. I explain that this strategy will aid them immensely in saving time and energy, giving them the ability to create an essay with some "pop." They are told that if they follow my technique, they only have to decide on three paragraphs versus five.

To illustrate my technique, I draw a large circle on the white board. Next I tell them a brief history that occurred in the 1960s:

During the Vietnam crisis, all males between the ages of 18-35 were required to register for military induction due to the Selective Service Act. Female were exempt. For most males, this meant a tour of Vietnam in which over 58,000 American died. Fast forward to the 21st-century and we have the Equal Rights Amendment, which for example, females doing the same job as her male counterparts, should receive the same wage. So, with this in mind, here is your essay prompt: (off to the side, I write down an essay prompt) *Should women be required to register for the military draft in the event of a World War?*

Some of your alpha males/females will start shouting out their feelings. I normally allow them to do so to stimulate those in the class that are a little more introvert. Then I begin my lecture on the "Bubble Method."

I point to the large circle and indicated that this is your first paragraph which is called the Thesis Statement. This is a fancy name to describe that this first-paragraph set the stage for all the writing that follows it. It is nothing more than a restatement of what you are going to write about. We know from the essay prompt I just wrote that you are being asked to take a position on the military drafting of women. So, give me some opening statements that might really "hook" the reader of your paper. Once I get some solid suggestions, I say, "Great, now we have our first paragraph pretty much done. Let's move on to our last paragraph at which point I draw a line from the large circle and place another circle. I go back to the large circle and place a P1, indication that this bubble is paragraph number one.

Inside the second circle I just drew, at the bottom I place a P2 for paragraph number 2. I add two more circles numbering them P3 and P4. Finally I draw a fifth circle placing P5 at the bottom and tell the class that this is your final paragraph – one of the easiest paragraphs to construct since here you will state your conclusions or summaries. "But, before we can decide on what should go into our final paragraph we have to see what goes into these other three empty circles."

Suggestions

To the side of my diagram, I draw a vertical line and place a + (positive sign) and a − (negative sign) on top of each column. Then I instruct the class that we will now do some brainstorming about the essay prompt. I ask them to raise their hands and state they feelings slowly since I will be recording their answers. Those that make statements in support of females being subject to the military draft go under the positive column: those opposed, under the negative column.

After praising them for a well-done job, I then take out a coin. I tell them that if, after I flip the coin, it comes up heads, we will take a positive position on the topic. A tails, the negative side.

After flipping the coin, I announce which side we will take and exam all the comments they made in the positive column and think about which of those would make the strongest paragraphs two through four. You will always have some students who don't like the their belief did not win on the issue but you respond as follows: *I appreciate that you are so passionate about your belief, but remember, the essay is graded not on which side of the issue you fall, but how well you construct the five-paragraph essay. What if you are given a prompt that you passionate about, but you can only come up with one or two statements, yet you have three to five counter-statements? You must use whichever side fills in the three bubbles with your strongest paragraphs.*

The beauty with the Bubble Technique is that struggling students will not feel overwhelmed after they realize that they don't have to do a lot of thinking to compose two of the five paragraphs since, regardless of the topic, they can easily write a paragraph about what their paper is all about and then, finally write the final paragraph wrapping it all up.

Science:

At the Alder Grove Academy, I broke science into three branches: Life Science, Earth Science and Physical Science (which contained Space Science). Having the students for an entire year, I could keep up a pace that allowed me to cover most of the basics for each branch.

Normally I started with Life Science followed by Earth and Physical Science. By the time the school year ended we covered at least the following:

Cell theory, animal vs. plant cells, the human body systems (circulatory, respiratory, digestive, excretory, nervous, endocrine, immune skeletal, muscle and reproductive), ecosystems, predator-prey relationships, water cycle, weather, biodiversity, genes, DNA, heredity, genetics, scientific method, scientific evidence, natural selection, structure and matter, energy (potential and kinetic) sound, plate tectonics, big bang theory, formation of the universe, planets, earth's structure, introduction to biology, zoology, and marine biology.

I created my own PowerPoints to illustrate my lectures as well as fill-in-the blank worksheets, quizzes and examinations. A lot to cover, but as you know your students you can modify your material as you see fit.

U.S. Government:

A book I enjoyed using to teach United States government was *The Everything American Government Book: From The Constitution To Present-Day Elections, All You Need To Understand Our Democratic System* Paperback – by Nick Ragoneby.

The Everything American Government Book unravels the complexities of our democracy and provides readers with the knowledge necessary to make the right decisions and take an active role in the management of their country. From the roots of American government and the challenges that have helped shape it over the years to its current structure and systems, this thoroughly researched work is ideal for anyone brushing up on civics, as well as students of all ages.

The book provides humor and excellent easy to understand examples of this complex topic. I used it to teach: the personalities and events that gave rise to our current system:The real significance of the Bill of Rights and the Constitution: The functions of each branch of government and how they work together and private sector's influence on public policy and decision-making. Finally it suggests ways to get involved and make a difference in politics. It is during U.S. Government, that I break the student up into manageable teams for a leaderless group exercise, although I do not tell them this in advance. I give each group copies of their assignment with a one-hour time frame for completion.

The topic: "*Most students hate school. Your group has been given the task of what a perfect school should be. You must be specific in bell schedule, courses to be taught, sports clubs, whatever you feel would be considered a great school.*" You must have someone take notes and select a person to report back on your suggestions. Democracy in action. Even your "at-risk" students will have a blast although be ready for some shouting and disagreements all around.

"At-risk" Incarcerated Adults

I've found that teaching incarcerated adults is very similar to "at-risk" incarcerated juveniles that I taught in our county's juvenile detention facility. In both institutions, you must be aware of your pencil count. A missing pencil could result in a lockdown of your classroom and a body search of your "students."

GED Social Studies:

In teaching my inmates GED Social Studies, I prepared a lesson plan from *Steck-Vaughn GED: Social Studies* (ISBN: 978-0739828342) showing an overview of the

Suggestions

topics that are likely to appear on the exam and well as discuss the layout of the exam questions. I then like to use portions of *Video Aided Instruction GED Review – Social Studies* which I purchased by calling or going online (1-800-238-1512). The DVDs you will receive will also include a download version of worksheets and quizzes. I stress to my inmate students that the layout of three of the GED exams (Social Studies, Language Arts, and Science) are very similar. In most cases I tell them to use the strategy of going straight to the questions, and then return to the narratives, graphs, charts, and pictures.

GED Reasoning Through Language Arts:

Again, using Steck-Vaughn *Reasoning Through Language Arts* (ISBN: 978-0739828366) I display a personally created PowerPoint showing the layout of the exam and the type of questions that will appear on their test. Using another set of DVDs I purchased from Video Aided Instruction (Language Arts), I stress the importance of reading the questions on the exam before doing the reading. I bring in many different types of articles showing my inmates how to read for content, extrapolate, draw conclusions – all the various types of questions they will encounter.

Once I feel that have the master of the above, I spend time teaching them my "Bubble Method" and have them write at least three, five-paragraphs essays in one week under time constraints similar to the exam.

GED Math:

In teaching GED math, I have found that two books compliment each other and supply my inmates with an ample supply of worksheets and activities to help prepare them for the GED math exam. *No Fear Math – All the Basics* (ISBN: 1-4114-0132-8) is an excellent book to use when reviewing basic math concepts. At the end of each chapter are quizzes of about 10 questions in length with the answers and explanations in the back.

For Algebra I used *California Mathematics Review* II published by the American Book Company (ISBN:978-1-59807-071-2). This book was original published as an aid to California teachers to help their high school students prepare for the now defunct California High School Exit Exam). The book goes way before what a person needs to master for their GED math exam, but it does an excellent job covering the Algebra and Plane Geometry problems they will face. Generally, with the use of these two books, I have my adult inmates (male and female) ready for their GED math test in five weeks.

Suggestions

GED Science:

I generally do not teach GED Science until the last few days of the six-week period since, as stated before, the strategy I recommend to the students is to skip the reading and focus first on the questions. A student who is solid in reading comprehension and charts and graphs interpretations with a little math (range calculation), usually passes this examination on their first try. I use, once again, a Steck-Vaughn GED Test Preparation book *GED Science* (ISBD: 978-0544274273). As a class, we review each chapter so that they see how the exam is laid out and to become familiar to the various ways data is shown such as charts, graphs, drawings, etc.

In conclusion, I hope you the reader, whether new to the profession or a veteran of many years in the classroom, found something(s) that might work in your classroom. Working with "at-risk" students, whether incarcerated or not, will be difficult but extremely rewarding. If any of my true stories inspired you, then I have done my job.

OTHER BOOKS
BY
GARY J. ROSE

Towards the Integration of Police Psychology Techniques to Reduce Juvenile Delinquency in our K-12 Classrooms
(ISBN:9781493556953)

Hitting Rock Bottom
(ISBN:9780998877709)

Ark of the Covenant – Raid on the Church of Our Lady Mary of Zion
(ISBN:9780998877730)

www.ingramcontent.com/pod-product-compliance
Lightning Source LLC
Chambersburg PA
CBHW071358160426
42811CB00111B/2225/J